WEALTH PROTECTION SECRETS

of a

MILLIONAIRE REAL ESTATE INVESTOR

WEALTH PROTECTION SECRETS
of a
MILLIONAIRE REAL ESTATE INVESTOR

WILLIAM BRONCHICK

Dearborn™
Trade Publishing
A **Kaplan Professional** Company

This publication is designed to provide accurate and authoritative information in regard to the subject matter covered. It is sold with the understanding that the publisher is not engaged in rendering legal, accounting, or other professional service. If legal advice or other expert assistance is required, the services of a competent professional person should be sought.

Vice President and Publisher: Cynthia A. Zigmund
Acquisitions Editor: Mary B. Good
Senior Managing Editor: Jack Kiburz
Interior Design: Lucy Jenkins
Cover Design: Design Alliance, Inc.
Typesetting: Elizabeth Pitts

Published by Dearborn Trade Publishing
A Kaplan Professional Company

Printed in the United States of America

03 04 05 10 9 8 7 6 5 4 3 2

Library of Congress Cataloging-in-Publication Data

Bronchick, William.
   Wealth protection secrets of a millionaire real estate investor /
William Bronchick.
      p.   cm.
Includes bibliographical references and index.
   ISBN 0-7931-7754-5 (pbk.)
1. Real estate investment—Law and legislation—United States—Popular
works. 2. Debtor and creditor—United States—Popular works. 3. Estate
planning—United States—Popular works. 4. Liability (Law)—United
States—Popular works.   I. Title.
   KF1079.Z9B76 2003
   346.7302—dc21

                                                          2003012909

CONTENTS

SECTION TWO
Appear Broke!

SECTION THREE
Control, Don't Own!

10. More Legal Issues   95

INTRODUCTION

We live in a lawsuit-happy society. Attorneys advertise on billboards with such slogans as *"Have you been injured? You may be entitled to a cash award!"* Nobody wants to accept responsibility for his or her own actions. Everybody is a victim.

I became involved in asset protection around 1990. Many of my clients were real estate investors who were running from creditors after the real estate and stock market crashes of the late 1980s. They came to me for help in holding off the creditors, foreclosures, and lawsuits. Unable to recover financially, many of them lost all of their assets and filed for bankruptcy protection.

The clients who made it through the crunch taught me a thing or two about financial survival. They were smart enough to arrange their business affairs in case of a crash. Nobody thinks about bankruptcy, business failure, lawsuits, and financial distress when times are good. However, as you will discover in this book, that is the *most* important time to think about it! You must have a plan for your wealth, or you may be destined to fail at the game we call "wealth preservation."

A Nationwide Epidemic

Eighty million lawsuits are filed every year, an average of 152 per minute. Chances are greater that you will be sued than that you will be in the hospital in the next year. The United States has 70 percent of the world's lawyers, and almost 50,000 new law school graduates are entering the profession each year! More lawyers mean more competition for clients, and that leads to new and creative theories of liability.

Here are some more interesting lawsuit facts:

- Contingency fees by trial lawyers exceed $10 billion annually.

- In personal injury litigation alone, over $96 billion is spent or lost each year in America to deliver $41 billion in compensation to injured parties and their attorneys.

- In a personal injury lawsuit, the average cost to defend yourself in a nonautomotive case is about $7,500.

(Source: Orange County Citizens Against Lawsuit Abuse—www.occala.org)

Theories of Liability

Civil liability comes in four basic categories: torts, breach of contract, strict liability, and vicarious liability.

Torts

Not to be confused with pastry tarts, a tort is a wrong or wrongful act committed on the person or property of another. The most common tort is *negligence,* the failure to act reasonably in light of the risk of harm to another. Negligent behavior can be an overt act or a failure to act when you should. Other torts include *misrepresentation of facts, infliction of emotional distress,* and *defamation of character.* These latter claims are usually based on *intentional* acts but are sometimes covered by liability insurance.

Breach of Contract

Breach of contract comprises a variety of claims, including failure to pay a debt or live up to an obligation, the result of which causes another harm. These types of claims are never covered by insurance, because they are always intentional in nature.

Strict Liability

Strict liability means that you are liable as a matter of law, even if you committed no overt act or were negligent. There is no defense for *"I didn't do anything wrong."*

Strict liability is usually statutory, which means it is governed by a specific state or federal law. For example, failure to pay withholding taxes on your employees results in your liability, even if your partner stole the money.

delegated , substitutionary

Vicarious Liability

In some cases, you may be vicariously liable for another's actions or inactions. The most common case is employers who are liable for the actions of their employees. Most states have laws that hold you liable if you lend someone your car and he or she gets into an accident, even if you weren't in the car. Also, you can be held liable for the actions of your business partners, even if you did nothing wrong.

Lawsuit and Asset Protection

At this point, I shall make a distinction between *lawsuit protection* and *asset protection*. Lawsuit protection is protecting *yourself* from personal liability. If a lawsuit is filed, are *you* liable or is some corporate entity taking the hit? If the plaintiff does obtain a court judgment against you, *what will they be able to collect?* Asset protection deals with the latter issue.

Plan Early

So when is the best time to start "planning" for a lawsuit? Before you get sued! Don't wait until you are sued to start moving around your assets. "CYA" does NOT mean "call your attorney." Lawsuit and asset protection is preventative maintenance. Nearly every state has some form of law that prohibits *fraudulent conveyances* (discussed in Chapter 10). A conveyance of property is fraudulent if it is intended to "delay, hinder, or defraud" creditors. The law gives creditors the right to ask a judge to put the property back into your name, so your creditors can take it away from you. So if you're thinking about transferring your assets to your spouse when you are threatened with a lawsuit, think again!

You can take some simple steps to reduce your risk of lawsuits and reduce your potential exposure to judgments. I call these steps the "ABCs of asset protection."

"A"—*Avoid* Lawsuits and Personal Liability

At the risk of insulting your intelligence, the best wealth protection strategy is DON'T GET SUED! I know this one is obvious, but some people just don't think about the potential liability they create as they conduct their affairs. It's called the "ostrich syndrome": Some people just stick their heads in the sand and pretend it won't happen to them. I want to give you a set of tools and a way of thinking that minimize your risk of liability.

The most obvious way to reduce your risk of liability is to stay home and watch television, which is not a realistic approach to life. However, being an "ostrich" is not a great way to live either. Somewhere in the middle, there is a point at which you will be comfortable knowing you are acting aggressively yet intelligently.

Even if you cannot avoid lawsuits, you can avoid being hit personally. This topic deals with lawsuit protection. If you do business in your own name, you will get sued personally. If you sign obligations personally, you are on the hook. Arrange your business affairs so that when things go bad, you are not personally on the hook. Use corporate entities to do business, so that you have a layer of protection between you and the liabilities your business creates.

"B"—Appear *Broke*

When I was first out of law school, my colleagues taught me how to carefully draft my documents so that all of my clients' rights would be protected. I used to love negotiating real estate contracts, because every lawyer had at least a ten-page addendum of items that he or she insisted on (which is why real estate brokers call lawyers "deal killers!").

After a while, reality sank in. The reality is that no matter what the paperwork says, the person who loses his or her money will sue those who walked away with the money. So after being involved in a lot of litigation over real estate and business disasters, I discovered this universal truth:

PEOPLE ONLY SUE OTHER PEOPLE WHO HAVE MONEY!

It's true, isn't it? Nobody is going to sue you if he or she thinks you have nothing from which to collect. This fact is especially true if someone retains a lawyer on a contingent-fee basis (i.e., the lawyer's fee is contingent on his or her ability to collect).

Let me give you a typical scenario of what happens in the lawsuit arena. Peter Plaintiff has a gripe against Donald Defendant. Peter thinks he should be able to collect. He goes to an attorney and is advised that he has a great case. The lawyer asks Peter for a nonrefundable $5,000 retainer to be applied toward the lawyer's regular hourly fee of $200. Like most people, Peter cannot afford the lawyer's fees, so he leaves the lawyer's office feeling dejected.

Peter continues his search for a more affordable lawyer, and while thumbing through the Yellow Pages, he sees a full page like this one:

Peter goes to Larry Lawyer for a free consultation. He tells Larry Lawyer his story. Larry knows that Donald Defendant's insurance won't cover the claim, so he needs to find a "deep pocket." After all, what good is a judgment if he can't collect?

Larry Lawyer begins to ask Peter about Donald Defendant's assets. Peter tells Larry about Donald's successful business and stock market holdings, which Donald always brags about. Peter also suspects that Donald owns a large apartment building across town. Larry jumps on the Internet and does a little digging in the public records. Lo and behold, he finds that Donald owns millions in real estate! It looks like Larry has a pot of gold waiting at the end of the rainbow, so he takes the case on a contingent-fee basis (i.e., Peter Plaintiff pays nothing up front, and Larry Lawyer collects his fee as a percentage of what he collects from Donald Defendant).

What if Peter Plaintiff knew nothing about Donald's assets, and a search of the public records came up empty? In that case, Larry Lawyer would probably ask Peter for a $5,000 retainer or tell him politely to hit the road. Lawyers don't like taking cases on a contingent-fee basis, unless they have a guaranteed way to collect the judgment. Contingent-fee lawyers don't get paid to sue; they get paid to collect! Peter Plaintiff is out of luck.

As you can see, appearing broke is one of the best ways to avoid lawsuits. If an attorney cannot find your assets with a cursory search of the public records, he or she probably won't bother to pursue the case. Johnson Wax couldn't make a better lawyer repellent in a can!

"C"—*Control* But Don't Own

John D. Rockefeller once said, "Own nothing, control everything." If you don't own anything, you have nothing to lose. Do you think Donald Trump has a bank account with several million dollars in cash? I doubt it. Even during the crash of his real estate empire, he was clever enough to retain some control over cash flow and maintain his flashy lifestyle. All the banks had to renegotiate with Trump. He was too resourceful to let go of all of his holdings.

So what we need are some flunkies to do our dirty work and take the fall. We call those flunkies:

- Corporations

- Limited partnerships

- Limited liability companies

If you operate your affairs so that you control your assets, but you don't own them, you will still have all the benefits of wealth without the risk of loss. Do you really care if you own all of your assets, or are you really interested in the perks of wealth (just ask your local congressperson!). So, strategy "C" is to move assets out of your name and into entities that you control. This is not a get-rich-quick book; it's a "get-broke-quick" book!

I want to make it clear at this time that I do not advocate that you break the law. In fact, I am advocating the exact opposite: I want you to follow the law in a way that benefits you. The law is on your side, if you know how to use it.

An important issue to keep in mind is that some wealth protection strategies will also minimize estate taxes or income taxes; however, not all lawsuit and asset protection techniques work together with estate or tax planning. For example, if your spouse owns all of your property, it may prevent you from losing it in a lawsuit, but you do lose the benefit of passing that property through your estate. Of course, there is a trade-off sometimes between asset protection and tax savings.

Asset protection, tax planning, and estate planning do go hand in hand if you utilize the principles properly. As with any estate or tax plan, you should seek competent, professional legal and tax advice before undertaking any of the ideas suggested in this book.

SECTION ONE

Avoid Lawsuits and Liability

Liabilities Affecting Your Personal and Family Affairs

Owning Property Jointly

Owning property jointly is one of the biggest pitfalls you can make from a lawsuit protection standpoint. The simple act of dividing up property between you and your spouse can be the difference between losing half of what you own and all of what you own.

Most married couples take real estate jointly when they buy. They do so because the bank or their Realtor® told them it should be that way. There's a danger in owning property jointly. Suppose the husband is a teacher and his wife is a doctor. He has a fairly low-risk occupation as far as lawsuits go. However, his wife has a very high-risk occupation. If she is sued, a creditor might be able to force the sale of the family home, since her name is on the title. In that scenario, it would be better for him to own the property solely in his own name (subject to community property rules, discussed below).

In some states, real estate held jointly by husband and wife cannot be attached by a creditor of one spouse (this is known as *tenancy by the entirety*). This strategy requires that both husband and wife wait it out until the creditor gives up or the debtor spouse dies first. If both husband and wife are young, the judgment will create a problem if they want to sell or refinance the property. Furthermore, the protection is lost if the couple is divorced and may not be afforded if one spouse files for bankruptcy protection.

The same rules apply for jointly held personal property. Elderly people commonly place their heirs jointly (as *joint tenants with right of survivorship*) on their bank accounts so when they die, the heirs inherit the money. The purpose for this arrangement is to pass the money quickly without the need for probate. In many circumstances, the law presumes bank accounts held in joint tenancy as each owning 100 percent, regardless of who actually contributed money to the account. Thus, if a creditor (especially the IRS) sued one of the heirs, the creditor might be able to attach all the money in the account, even if the debtor contributed no money to the account! Even if the non-debtor could prove which portion of the property was his or hers, a creditor can still force the sale of the asset to attach the debtor's share. This type of "distress" sale will wreak havoc on the nondebtor's equity, because assets usually sell for a fraction of their value at these sales.

A trust can help accomplish the same goals without exposing the money to the creditors of the heirs. For bank accounts, ask your branch manager about a POD (payable on death) account. It accomplishes the same task without the formality and expense of a written trust agreement.

Finally, in states where there is *community property* (California, Louisiana, Texas, Wisconsin, Idaho, Arizona, Nevada, New Mexico, and Washington), all property of husband and wife acquired after the marriage is presumed to belong to both, regardless of how it is titled. Thus, a creditor can usually attack all of the marital property, even if only one spouse is liable for the debt. It may be desirable to convert community property in writing to "separate" property, then divide up the property between the spouses according to their risk of getting sued. In the event of a lawsuit, the couple could prove which property is the separate property of the nondebtor spouse. A sample agreement of this type is included in the Appendix.

> **Important Note on Community Property**
>
> Community property and joint ownership rules differ from state to state. You should consult with a qualified attorney in your state about the possible estate planning, capital gains, and gift tax issues involved in dividing up jointly held property.

Divorce

Statistics show that more than 50 percent of marriages end in divorce. The most difficult issue in a divorce can be the division of property. The general rule in most states is that property acquired by the couple after they are married is the property of both. (In some states it is called equitable distribution; in other states it is called community property. There is a subtle legal difference between the two for purposes of legal ownership and tax issues, but the net result is generally the same for long-term marriages when property is distributed on divorce.) This rule also applies to property that belongs to one spouse but increases in value during the marriage. "Property" can also include the value of a professional practice or business to which the spouse directly or indirectly contributed.

"Prenups"

Notwithstanding the above-stated rules, spouses can make any agreement they wish in writing to the contrary. These agreements, of course, are subject to public policy restrictions that vary from state to state (for example, in most states a spouse cannot be disregarded in a will; the law automatically gives the surviving spouse a share, called an "elective share," even if he or she was excluded).

Generally speaking, there are two types of such agreements: premarital agreements and postmarital agreements. Many people are reluctant to enter into premarital agreements (also known as prenuptial or antenuptial agreements) for fear that their soon-to-be spouse may be insulted. However, in a second marriage situation an individual may want to make certain that children from a previous marriage are provided for, and therefore, such an agreement may be necessary. In order for such an agreement to be enforceable, full disclosure of both spouses' assets must be made to each in writing. In addition, both spouses should be represented by their own attorneys and sign an acknowledgment that each understands the legal and financial ramifications of such an agreement.

A postmarital agreement (also called a postnuptial agreement) is made after the couple is married. It is an agreement that may define which property is the separate property of each spouse. It may also be an agreement to convert marital property into the separate property of either spouse. These agreements are generally enforceable and may be effective to protect the nondebtor spouse against the creditors of the debtor spouse.

Credit Issues

Finally, there is the practical side of divorce. If you are the primary cardholder, guarantor, or signatory on debt, remove your spouse from these accounts if you are not in communication. Divorces often result in bad credit, because an angry spouse decides to get even by charging up a storm. If you are no longer in communication with your spouse, contact all of your creditors and let it be known that you will not be responsible for any additional debt incurred by your ex-spouse.

Liability for Mortgage Loan

As part of a divorce settlement, it is common for one spouse to receive title to the marital residence. In most cases, both parties signed the original mortgage note. What few people realize is that transferring title to the property does *not* remove your obligation on the note. Furthermore, if the other spouse defaults on the payments, you have absolutely no way to get the property back!

Consider selling the property on divorce or inserting a provision in the settlement agreement that requires your ex-spouse to refinance the mortgage loan within a six-month time period. If your ex-spouse is unwilling or unable to qualify for a new loan, keep your name on the deed or have your ex-spouse sign a security instrument (second mortgage or deed of trust) that allows you to foreclose the property if he or she defaults on the first mortgage loan. In this case, you will have recourse against the property if your ex-spouse defaults on the payment obligation.

Improper Use of a Living Trust

Living trusts are being touted by some financial planners as an asset protection device. While revocable living trusts can help you avoid probate, they provide little or no protection from creditors of the grantor/beneficiary (discussed in Chapter 6).

Do not title all your assets in the name of your living trust! If you title all of your assets into a living trust, and your living trust is sued, all of your assets are at risk; for example, if your automobile is titled in the living trust and is involved in an accident, your living trust can be sued as a defendant. It is recommended that you own your "risky" assets (i.e., those assets that create liability, such as a business, automobile, or a boat) in a corporation first, and then have the shares of your corporation owned by your living trust. See Figure 1.1. That way, if the corporation is sued, the creditor or plaintiff is limited to the assets of the corporation.

For married couples, living trusts do provide limited protection for the nondebtor spouse from creditors of the debtor spouse, because the living trust may be a vehicle for dividing up the assets of the

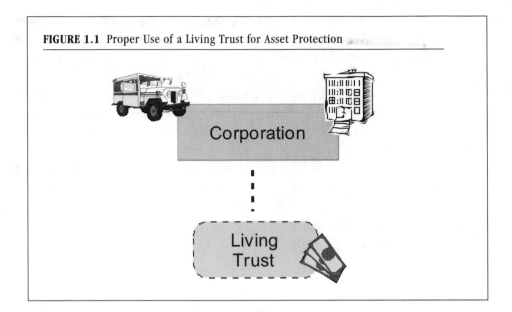

FIGURE 1.1 Proper Use of a Living Trust for Asset Protection

couple. Typically, a living trust will list the assets of the couple in the form of a "schedule." If the husband were sued, the wife could prove that certain assets belonged solely to her living trust and thus would be beyond reach of the husband's creditors (estate planning experts suggest that each spouse have his or her own living trust for this purpose). A sample living trust agreement can be found in the Appendix.

Living trusts may be effective in keeping your ownership of assets private, if title is held in the name of a trustee other than you or your spouse. This strategy will be discussed in more detail in Section Two.

Letting Kids Drive Your Car

Few people realize that in most states, the registered owner of a motor vehicle is personally liable for any accidents that happen while someone else is driving his or her car. If you have children, you can lose it all in one night if they are in an accident and seriously injure another. A simple joyride can lead to bankruptcy and losing everything you worked hard for. If you buy your kids a car, register the car in their name, not yours. If you permit your kids to drive your car, make certain you have lots of insurance! Remember: Most insurance companies won't pay claims for injuries because of a DUI accident.

Failing to Keep Adequate Insurance

Don't be cheap. Insurance will protect you in 90 percent of all circumstances. If you keep the minimum automobile insurance, increase the liability limits. You can increase your automobile liability insurance from $250,000 to $1,000,000 for a relatively small amount. Keep in mind that if your automobile insurance is not adequate to cover the claim, the injured party can go after your personal assets for the difference. If you have several automobiles and a business, you should consider an umbrella policy that will kick in after your homeowners, business, or automobile policy is exhausted.

Note on Umbrella Policies

Umbrella insurance covers more money, not more claims. If you have a $250,000 policy on your automobile and a $2,000,000 umbrella policy, you will have a lot of coverage for your car. However, if the automobile policy does not cover the claim, neither does the umbrella policy.

Insurance also gives you an attorney in an event you are sued, even if the claim is settled before trial. The duty of an insurer to defend (pay for your lawyer) is much broader than its duty to indemnify (pay for claims against you). Even if the lawsuit is completely bogus, the insurance company will provide you with a lawyer, saving you thousands of dollars. And, because most cases are settled before trial, there is little or no cost to you. Insurance does not cover all disputes, so consider a prepaid legal plan, especially if you have your own business.

Cosigning a Loan

If you want to keep friends, don't cosign loans for them. If they default, you are liable. They will ruin your credit as well as their own. If they can't qualify for the loan, they should save and pay cash, as our parents used to do.

If you do sign for someone else, you should be aware of the difference between "cosigning" and "guaranteeing" a debt. In most states, a cosigner is jointly and severally liable with the primary signatory. This means that the creditor can go after either party for the full amount in the event of default. Furthermore, a cosigner's credit report usually reflects late payments.

A guarantor is secondarily liable if the primary signatory defaults. Thus, the creditor must exhaust his or her remedies against the primary signatory before proceeding against the guarantor. In some states, the law makes no distinction between a cosigner and a guarantor. Credit reporting agencies often fail to make the distinction, so a late payment by the other signer will adversely affect your credit.

"Social Host" Liability

Certain states will hold the host of a party and/or the owner of the premises liable for an automobile accident caused by an intoxicated person who was served alcohol at their house. If you own a business, your business can be held liable, even if the party was held away from the premises of your regular business. Check your state laws to determine how social host liability may affect your personal or business parties. You can download a state-by-state report on the Internet at <http://faceproject.securedata.net/socialhostliabilitylaws.html>.

Dog Bites

Dogs are personal property, so you are liable for the actions of your pets. In some states, there is a one-bite rule, which means that once your dog bites someone, you are on notice that he has a propensity for aggression. In other states, the liability for pets is *absolute*, which means that if someone is injured by your dog, he or she need not prove that you were at fault, only that you are the owner.

Damages caused as a result of your dog are not limited to bites. For example, if your dog runs into the street and causes a car accident, you may be liable. If someone falls down and is injured because your dog startled him or her, you are liable, even if your dog was on a leash.

There isn't a lot you can do to protect yourself from liability in these cases. Act responsibly, keep your dog trained and on a controlled leash, and post a "beware of dog" sign on your property. Also, check your state and local laws on pet ownership to determine which activities (or failures to act) will result in strict (or other) liability. For more information and recent developments on dog bite law, visit <www.dogbitelaw.com>.

Children

Natural inclinations

Liability for your children's actions is similar to the one-bite rule: If you are aware of your child's propensity for a certain type of behavior and do nothing to correct it, you may be liable for your child's wrongful actions. The theory of liability is essentially "negligent parenting." The one exception is liability for use of your automobile, which usually results in strict liability (you are liable for children's automobile accidents whether or not you acted reasonably).

Reporting Incidents to the Insurance Company

I have seen many people suffer unnecessarily because they fail to report minor incidences to their insurance company. They usually fail to report out of ignorance or fear that their insurance premiums will go up. Here is the pitfall: Most insurance policies contain a provision that denies coverage if the incident is not timely reported.

If you have a professional malpractice policy, this issue is especially relevant. Even if an incident occurs that might lead to liability, you are obligated to report these facts promptly. If you do not report these facts and are sued a year later, your insurance company will not even give you a lawyer to defend the claim. Thus, you will have to pay for your own lawyer to defend what may be a bogus lawsuit. Always report an incident to your insurance company in a timely manner. Insurance companies hate to pay claims, but don't give them an excuse not to!

Failing to "Put It in Writing"

Always leave a paper trail. Whenever you speak with someone at a company, the IRS, or any governmental organization, get it in writing. If they won't give it to you in writing, send them a "self-serving" follow-up letter summarizing your conversation. Their failure to object to its contents may be deemed an admission of what the letter states. Keep a copy in your file in case you have to prove the oral conversation in court.

If you have a contract in writing and you modify the terms of the contract orally, get it in writing. If you want an estimate for repairs on your car, your dishwasher, your hot water heater, or your roof, get it in writing. If you settle a claim or potential lawsuit for money, get it in writing (and get a signed "release"). Remember: It's not what happens, it's what you can prove in court (also known as the "O.J. rule")! The written word is your most powerful weapon in court, so use it.

Opening Your Mouth Too Wide

If you don't want to be held liable, admit nothing, deny everything, and never reduce anything to writing. It's their word against yours. If you get upset and write a nasty letter, watch what you say. If you are involved in what could potentially be a lawsuit, think before you act. Do not write offensive letters to your adversary stating your legal positions. Successful litigation involves some element of surprise. State firmly but vaguely that you intend to pursue your legal remedies—that's all!

As an attorney, I have used this strategy very effectively on the defense. Attorneys always threaten to sue for everything in an attempt to get you to settle. Before offering a settlement, see if the other attorney is bluffing or really has a case. Because most attorneys love to argue and be "right," I simply fax a letter asking them what my client has done wrong. Invariably, the other attorney takes the bait and faxes me back a six-page letter outlining everything. If the attorney's case is based on mere allegations, I call his bluff.

CHAPTER 2

Liabilities Affecting Small Businesses

According to recent studies, only about 35 percent of small businesses survive the first year. Most small businesses require the owners to put up cash and sign personally for debts, which is a recipe for disaster. Let's look at some of the common mistakes small business operators make and how to remedy them.

Doing Business as a Sole Proprietor

Most people who go into business do so as a sole proprietor. *Sole proprietorship* means doing business in your own name or under a *d/b/a* (doing business as). Most people do business in this fashion, because it is easy and requires no formalities. However, this form of business is also one of the most dangerous.

The sole proprietorship offers absolutely no lawsuit protection and is at higher risk of audit (statistically, the chances of a small business being audited are far greater as a sole proprietor than as a corporation). There is no legal distinction between a sole proprietor and his or her business. If the business incurs an obligation or is sued, all of the individual's personal assets (in addition to business assets) are at risk. For less than $100 in most states, you can form a corporation to conduct your business or trade. If properly maintained, a corporation will shield your personal assets from lawsuits or bankruptcy.

Doing Business with Partners

Doing business with a partner is even worse than doing business as a sole proprietor. A *partnership* is formed when two or more people decide to do business together for profit. It does not require a formal partnership agreement or the filing of any official documents, although it is often done that way. A partnership can be created even if you did not intend it (discussed below)!

Here is the problem with partnerships: If your partner does something stupid, you are liable. If you allow your partner to commit the partnership to a contract, the partnership and its partners can be held liable for that debt. If your partner slanders another, commits a negligent act, or incurs a debt on behalf of the partnership, you are on the hook—even if your partner files bankruptcy! This is called the doctrine of *joint and several liability.* Regardless of the percentage of fault between you and your partners, a judgment by a creditor for any wrongful acts is 100 percent collectible from any one of the partners. Joint and several liability can be particularly disastrous if you are the "silent" partner with all of the money.

Another problem is the "accidental" partnership. Let's say that Harry finds a good business deal. He needs capital, so he approaches Fred. Fred agrees to invest with Harry. Fred is the silent partner. Harry deals with the public, referring to his partner Fred. Fred and Harry do business, make money, and part ways. A month later, Harry gets into financial trouble. Creditors come knocking on his door, but he has no money to pay. The creditors then come after his partner Fred. Is Fred liable? In some cases, the answer is "yes," if the public thought Harry and Fred were partners and Fred did nothing to stop Harry from leading people to believe they were partners.

If you only want to do a "one shot" deal, consider drafting a *joint venture agreement.* A joint venture is basically a partnership for a specific purpose. A sample joint venture agreement can be found in the Appendix. If you intend to do business with partners long term, consider a corporation, limited partnership, or limited liability company.

Finally, if you are a professional, consider a limited liability partnership, or LLP. Many states allow a general partnership to register as an LLP for a small fee. The registered LLP does not always protect partners for general debts of the partnership, but it will shield the partners for the wrongdoings of its partners. However, it will not protect you from liability for your own wrongdoings.

Using a Corporation Improperly

Using a corporation improperly is probably one of the biggest mistakes people make in business. They pay an attorney $500 to $1,000 to file a corporation, then they take the corporation book and stick it in the closet. A corporation will not shield you from personal liability if you do not follow corporate formalities! A court can set aside the corporate "shield" and permit litigants to go after the shareholders personally. Even worse, if the IRS audits you, it can set aside the corporation and hold you personally liable for the taxes!

Corporate formalities involve, at a minimum, the following:

- Filling out the corporate minutes book

- Electing a board of directors and officers

- Issuing stock certificates

- Obtaining an employer identification number (EIN). See the Appendix for a sample IRS Form SS-4 for applying for an EIN.

- Opening a bank account in the corporation's name

- Holding yearly shareholders and directors meetings

- Funding your corporation with sufficient operating capital

- Keeping proper corporate records

These activities will take, at best, two hours a year. They don't have to be formal, but they must be documented. (Visit <www.legal wiz.com> for information on do-it-yourself kits for setting up and operating your own corporation, or see the Resources at the end of this book.)

Failing to Designate Your Corporate Capacity

If you take the time and expense to form and maintain a corporation, why would you sign personally on all of its obligations? If you fail to sign in the proper capacity *just once,* you may be held liable for your personal signature.

If you are the president of the corporation, sign all of your letters, checks, contracts, etc., in the proper capacity (e.g., John Smith, President). I can't tell you how many times I've seen a business card that reads, ABC Corporation, John Smith, Owner. The owners of a corporation are its shareholders; shareholders cannot represent the corporation, only the officers. It is possible for you to be *both* shareholder and officer; just make sure it's clear which role you are playing. If you want the IRS or the court to treat you like a corporation, then act like one. Sign your name in the capacity in which you are acting.

Just recently a contract was handed to me that had my name with a slash and my company name. I simply added the words *secretary of* between the two names to make it clear I was signing as an officer, not jointly with the corporation. If it is not clear whether you are signing as an officer of the corporation or as an individual offering a personal guarantee, the law will always rule against you.

A final point worth mentioning is that you should make certain that your signs, letterhead, business cards, and other marketing items state that you are a corporation. Remember to include the *Inc., Corp.,* or *Ltd.* designation at the end of your business name. Leave no doubt that your company is a corporation.

Avoid using your surname in your company name (e.g., John Smith Company), so there is no confusion to your customers. Also, if you sell your business or the corporation goes bankrupt, you don't want your name tied to it!

Personally Guaranteeing Corporate Liabilities

If you have a new business that is a corporation, you are often asked to pledge your personal signature to guarantee the corporation's debts. By doing this, you are risking all of your assets if the business fails, even if the corporation files for bankruptcy.

In some situations, such as a bank loan or line of credit, it is inevitable that you must sign personally. However, it is not necessary to give a personal guarantee in every situation, simply because it is requested. Often, vendors of your business will request that you sign a personal guarantee of a corporate liability. If they are not extending you credit, you should simply refuse. For example, if a landlord requests a personal guarantee on a lease, offer a larger security deposit instead. Or, you can negotiate so that after two years of prompt payment, your personal guarantee is not necessary. If you decide to sell your business, keep in mind that your personal guarantee on the lease will continue after you assign your lease to the new owner.

If you have signed personal guarantees in the past on corporate obligations, write a letter to the business requesting that your personal guarantee be removed. If you have been doing business for at least two years with the company, it should have no problem with removing your personal name, especially if the business has good liquidity and credit. (You may want your company to become a member of Dun & Bradstreet [D&B] for this purpose—<www.dandb.com>.)

Allowing Your Spouse to Cosign

It's bad enough that you have to sign personally and pledge all of your assets. Why should your spouse be so foolish as well? In most non-community-property states, spouses are not liable for each other's debts. Therefore, the nonliability of the spouse is sometimes the only saving grace when a business fails.

Suppose that your wife has a business in which she is required to borrow money with a personal guarantee. It may be years later that the business fails, and she is stuck with the debt. Meanwhile, she should consider quietly transferring assets out of her name and into her husband's name (not while facing a lawsuit, of course, because that is considered a fraudulent conveyance; discussed in Chapter 10). This strategy presumes that the husband is not in a situation in which he may have a potential liability problem. In most community-property states, one spouse's property can be used to satisfy the other's debts. In these situations, it may be advisable to place personal assets into an irrevocable trust to protect them from creditors.

Paying Yourself before Covering Your Payroll

If your business is short on cash or pending bankruptcy, pay your employees before you pay other creditors. In many states, the law holds you personally liable for unpaid wages, even if you have a corporation. Payroll taxes are the responsibility of all officers, directors, and "responsible parties."

These obligations are not dischargeable in Chapter 7 bankruptcy. Ordinary debts, on the other hand, are not chargeable to corporate officers, directors, and shareholders and *are* dischargeable in bankruptcy. If your company is in trouble, cover payroll *first* and ordinary debts second.

Using Copyrighted Material

Federal copyright laws are old, archaic, and obsolete. They are still the law, however. If you use a slogan, photo, name, logo, or other unique symbol identified with another company, you can be held civilly and possibly criminally liable. If you sell another company's product and place its logo in your advertising or in your windows without its permission, you can be sued for copyright infringement. If you play music in your place of business without permission, you can be sued for copyright infringement. If you own a restaurant or bar with live music, you cannot have musicians playing copyrighted songs without permission.

Copyright infringement is so broad and so blatantly violated on a daily basis that most business liability insurance policies will cover you. Check with your insurance carrier to make certain that it covers you for copyright, patent, and trademark violations.

Failing to Delineate Carefully between Employees and Independent Contractors

This area is one of the most dangerous for doing business. The IRS and your state department of labor are on the lookout for employers that don't collect and pay withholding taxes, unemployment, and/or workers' compensation insurance.

If you have employees who are "off the books," you are looking for trouble. If you get caught, you will have to pay the withholding taxes and as much as a 25 percent penalty. Intentionally failing to file W-2 forms will subject you to a $100 fine per form. The fine for failure to complete INS Form I-9 is from $100 to $1,000 per form. The corporation will not shield you from liability in this case either. All officers, directors, and/or responsible parties are personally liable for the taxes, and this obligation is NOT dischargeable in bankruptcy.

If you have people who do "contract" work for you on a per diem basis, they may be considered "employees" by the IRS. If workers fail to pay their estimated taxes, you may still be liable for withholding. If these workers are under your control and supervision and only do work for you, the IRS may consider them employees, even if *you* don't. If this happens, you may be liable for back taxes and penalties as described above.

If you want to protect yourself, at a minimum you should:

- Hire only corporate contractors (or have a business card and letterhead of an unincorporated contractor).

- Require proof of insurance in writing (liability, unemployment, and workers' compensation).

- Have a written contract or estimate on the worker's letterhead that states he or she will work his or her own hours and that you will have no direct supervision over the details of the work (see sample agreement in the Appendix).

- Have letters of reference from other people the person did work for in your file to show that he or she did not work solely for you.

- File IRS Form 1099 for every worker or unincorporated business to whom you pay more than $600 per year.

Also included in the Appendix is a copy of IRS Form SS-8, which is used to determine whether an individual is an employee or independent contractor.

In addition to possible tax implications, an independent contractor can create liability for you if a court determines that the contractor is your "employee." For example, if your "independent" contractor is negligent and injures another, the injured party can sue you directly. If facts show that you exercised enough control over your contractor, a court may rule that this contractor is your employee for liability purposes. As you may know, an employer is "vicariously" liable for the acts of his or her employees (i.e., liable as a matter of law without proof of fault on the part of the employer). Make certain you follow the above guidelines for hiring contractors, particularly regarding the issue of "control."

Finally, be aware under your state law which duties are considered "inherently dangerous." These duties cannot be delegated to an independent contractor without liability on your part, regardless of whether the person you hire is considered an independent contractor or an employee.

Employee Lawsuits

Employees not only can create liability *for* you, they also can create liability *against* you. Employee discrimination, wrongful termination, and sexual harassment suits are at an all-time high. The worse news is that many of these lawsuits are not covered by liability insurance. Following is a brief summary of issues to look out for.

Discrimination Issues

In hiring, advertising for, and promoting employees, you cannot usually discriminate on the basis of race, color, religion, national origin, age, gender, disability, marital or pregnancy status, and sexual orientation (check your state law for additional or different restrictions; as of the date of the first printing of this book, California is proposing a transgender discrimination law).

Wrongful Termination

These lawsuits are typically filed in the nature of a "breach of contract" claim; for example, an employee was promised continued employment and was prematurely fired. In other cases, the employee may claim that the employer did not follow proper procedure in terminating the employee as stated in company policy manuals or an employment contract. To make matters simple, you may consider requiring that all new employees sign an acknowledgment that their employment is "at will" (so long as the employer wants to retain the employee's services).

Sexual Harassment

Sexual harassment is a form of sex discrimination and is illegal under both state and federal laws. The most obvious harassment is called "quid pro quo" harassment. In this case, the employer demands sexual favors in return for a raise or promise not to fire.

The more subtle harassment occurs when an employer permits activity that constitutes an abusive or "hostile" working environment. Unwelcome advances, demeaning jokes, and inappropriate comments on attire have all been considered forms of sexual harassment. Be aware of what goes on in your business. Have written policies concerning unacceptable conduct in the workplace. Have a complaint system and investigate all claims promptly.

Employer liability (also known as Human Resources law) is too vast a topic to cover summarily, so it is suggested that you research this topic further if you have employees in your business. Two excellent books on the topic are *Stay out of Court: The Manager's Guide to Preventing Employee Lawsuits* by Rita Risser (Prentice Hall, 1993) and *The Employer's Legal Handbook* by Fred Steingold (Nolo Press, 2003).

CHAPTER 3

Liabilities Affecting Property Owners and Landlords

Owning Real Estate in Your Own Name

You wouldn't walk around with a financial statement taped to your forehead would you? So why would you have your most valuable assets exposed to public scrutiny?

Owning real estate in your own name is like walking around with a giant "kick me" sign taped to your back. In every county in the United States, copies of deeds to real estate are recorded in the public records. Anyone can go down to the county courthouse or recorder's office and look up the owner of any property in the county. Mortgages on properties will be recorded as well. Most recorded mortgages will state the amount of the original principal balance and the date the mortgage payments began. All someone has to do is figure out the balance of your mortgage (using a financial calculator) and subtract that amount from the market value of your house. Bingo! Now they know how much equity you have, and hence whether suing you is worthwhile.

Remember the example we discussed earlier about the contingency-fee lawyer? The scenario is absolutely accurate. Most contingency-fee lawyers will not take a case unless they think there is something on which to collect. If you have no real estate in your name, then finding out your ownership interest will not be easy for a typical lawyer. It's not that most lawyers are lazy or dense (you can decide without my opinion), it's simply a matter of allocation of resources. Lawyers focus on cases they can win and on which they can collect. If they don't find real estate in your name (and no other apparent "deep pocket" exists), they probably won't take the case on a contingency-fee basis.

There is another problem with owning real estate in your own name. If a judgment or IRS lien is obtained against you and filed in the county in which you own real estate, all real estate in that county will have a lien attached to it. You cannot sell or refinance a property in that county, since no title insurance company will issue a clean title. Without title insurance, no bank will approve a loan. No bank, no buyer. You're stuck until you pay off the lien.

Here is what happens next. If you live in a state that does not have a homestead exemption (only a handful have unlimited homestead exemptions that protect your home from creditor attachment; see the Appendix for a list), a judgment creditor can put your property up for sale at a sheriff's auction to the highest bidder. And you can bet your bottom dollar that the amount your house will sell for will be less than market value.

Now that I've given you that wake-up call, I'll give you a few solutions. First, don't hold title in your name. If you have rental property, hold title to land in the name of your corporation, trust, or limited liability company. Of course, there are practical considerations. If you have a mortgage on the property, any transfer of property can trigger the "due on sale" clause of the mortgage. In that case, the lender can call the full amount of the loan due. However, federal law provides an exemption for transferring title into an *intervivos* trust, such as an "Illinois-type" land trust (12 U.S.C. Sec.1701j-3(d)(8)). We will discuss this strategy in more detail in Section Two.

A land trust, if properly set up and implemented, will hide your name from the public records. No one will know who owns the property but you, your attorney, and the trustee. If a judgment is entered against you, the lien will not automatically attach to the property, because the title is not in your name. (For more information on how to set up and use land trusts, visit my Web site at <www.legalwiz.com>.)

Failing to Maintain Your Property and Boundaries

If you own a house or building that borders a public walkway, you are under a legal obligation to keep your property and right-of-way free from obstacles and defects that can cause injury. If you run a business that has a storefront, you may be obligated to keep the sidewalk free from debris, snow, and ice.

If you have a house with a swimming pool, you are obligated to maintain a fence around your property. In some cities, there are ordinances that require a certain type and size of fence. A Florida jury recently awarded $100 million in damages against a landlord after a child drowned in a pool that was not properly fenced. If you have a dog, you are liable for any injury or damages your dog causes to another, even if the dog got out of the house by accident. Remove or isolate any "attractive nuisances" on your property that invite young children. Attractive nuisances are dangerous conditions or activities that tend to attract children who may not appreciate the dangers involved. A swimming pool is an obvious attractive nuisance, but more common items (such as a seated lawn mower or a snowmobile) may be dangerous if left in the hands of a minor.

If you have a walkway on your property that you regularly permit the public to cross (even passively), you can be held liable for any injury on that right-of-way. Posting a no-trespassing sign will not shield you from liability, if people regularly ignore the sign. A known or anticipated trespasser is treated the same under the law as a "licensee"— you have a duty to warn the public about known, dangerous conditions that are not readily apparent. If you don't want this obligation, you should physically obstruct your property with a fence or other means to prevent access.

Overhanging Branches

If you have branches that hang over your neighbor's yard, you are liable if the branches hurt someone or cause damage to your neighbor's property. If the tree is close to the property line, ownership of the tree is determined by who has the trunk of the tree on his side. If you are uncertain about the property line, have a professional survey done (a lot cheaper than removing a tree!).

Criminal Activity

Finally, if you own rental property, especially multiunit buildings in high-crime neighborhoods, be aware of who your property manager is renting to. Further, be aware of any persistent criminal activities that occur in your building. You may be held civilly liable for criminal activities that occur on your premises, even if an outsider perpetrated the crime. If your building has frequent security problems, take steps to rectify these conditions, or you may be held liable for criminal acts on your tenants. In some states, if there is persistent illegal activity in your building, the government can actually seize your property and condemn the building for up to a year!

Allowing Someone to Assume Your Loan

If you purchased a home with a freely assumable FHA or VA mortgage, do not allow someone to take over your loan without qualifying. Most FHA mortgages originated before 1989 and VA mortgages originated before 1987 are freely assumable, which means you can transfer title and permit someone else to take over the loan. However, the assumption by a third party does not always absolve you from liability. If your loan is assumed by another party without the lender *qualifying* that party, you are still responsible for that loan. If the new party defaults and the property is foreclosed, you and anyone else who originated and/or assumed that loan will be liable for any deficiency balance.

The solution is as follows: If you originated the loan, make certain that the new buyer qualifies for the loan. If the buyer has poor credit, have an agreement that he or she will refinance within a two-year time period. For security, you can always sell on an installment land contract and hold the deed as security until he or she refinances.

If you plan to purchase a property by assuming a nonqualifying loan, you do not have to assume the loan in your name. You can take title in a corporation or trust and have the corporation or trust assume responsibility for the loan.

Fair Housing Issues

If you own rental property, fair housing laws can get you into trouble. Make certain that you understand these laws. Under federal law (42 U.S.C. Sec. 3601–3619, 3631), you cannot discriminate based on race, color, religion, national origin, familial status (which includes marital status and having children), age, or sex. The rules apply not only to the screening process but also to the words you use in advertising the property.

Most people are aware that they cannot discriminate against potential renters based on race, sex, color, national origin, or religious beliefs. Many landlords are not aware that states, and even some localities, have additional restrictions on discrimination. For example, California, Minnesota, and North Dakota prohibit discrimination based on source of income. In these states, you cannot deny an applicant solely because he or she is receiving public assistance.

Most landlords don't intentionally discriminate, and when they do so, it is in a more subtle manner. Here are a few examples:

- If you take two applications from an unmarried couple and one from a married couple, this may be considered discrimination based on marital status.

- If a family of six is applying to rent a two-bedroom condominium, you cannot turn them away, because this would be discrimination based on familial status.

- If you only ask Hispanic people for proof of citizenship, you are discriminating based on national origin.

There is no way to protect yourself from these violations other than to learn the law. Go to your public library or attend a seminar in your community. In addition, check your state, county, and city for additional restrictions on discrimination in housing, such as age, source of income (e.g., welfare), political affiliation, and sexual orientation. You can find more information on housing discrimination laws on the Internet at <www.fairhousing.com>.

Environmental Liability

If you are purchasing a commercial business or building, make certain that you have a complete and thorough inspection of the premises by a trained environmental expert. Federal law holds the owner liable for environmental cleanups, even if you did not create the condition. A corporation's officers and directors can be held *personally* liable for environmental violations and be fined thousands of dollars. In addition, be aware of state and federal lead-based paint disclosure laws if you are renting or selling your property. (Call 800-424-LEAD for more information.)

Americans with Disabilities Act

The Americans with Disabilities Act (ADA) also prohibits you from discriminating against people with a disability. Of course, no decent human being would turn someone down because he or she was in a wheelchair. However, the definition of the word *disability* goes way beyond physical disability. A person with a mental disability is covered by the ADA, as is an alcoholic undergoing treatment or a person convicted of prior drug use. The ADA does exclude drug dealers, however. The catch-22 is that if you have drug addicts as tenants, they tend to attract drug dealers and other criminal activities!

SECTION TWO

Appear Broke!

Using Trusts for Privacy

Appearing broke is one of the best ways to avoid lawsuits. Remember the earlier example of the contingency-fee attorney? If the attorney cannot find some assets with a cursory search of the public records, he or she probably will not take the case on a contingent-fee basis. Instead, the attorney will insist on a large retainer fee and charge by the hour. Most people cannot afford litigation attorneys by the hour, so you win the game.

Use Land Trusts to Hide Your Real Estate

A land trust is an arrangement by which title to land is conveyed to a trustee to hold for the benefit of another (the beneficiary). The creator of the trust is called the "settlor" (in some states, "grantor" or "trustor"). The settlor usually remains the beneficiary for life, and his or her interests under the trust pass to another on death. The beneficiary of a land trust has the absolute right to direct and control the trustee and receive all income from the trust. As far as the world is concerned, the trustee is the owner of the property, with the complete power to lease, mortgage, or sell the property. However, his or her power is restricted by the trust agreement with the beneficiary. A land trust is also known as a "title holding" or "nominee" trust, because the trustee is really just an appointed person holding title to the property for the beneficiary. The trustee has no function other than to do what the beneficiary directs.

A land trust is revocable; it can be changed, modified, or terminated while the settlor is still alive. If the trustee becomes uncooperative, the beneficiary can terminate him or her and appoint a new trustee. The trust property is being held by the trustee as a fiduciary, so the trustee has no personal liability for simply being on the title.

A land trust is not a new or novel idea. The history of land trusts can be traced back hundreds of years to the times of feudal England. During the reign of King Henry VIII, owning realty as a citizen was considered somewhat of a liability. If you owned land in your name, you had two major obligations: pay handsome taxes to the King and serve in the King's army. Of course, wherever there are burdensome laws, there are creative lawyers.

People of that time saw the opportunity in hiding or masking ownership of property. They began transferring title to relatives and friends to remove their names from the public records. They also titled real estate in the name of a relative or trusted friend in "trust" for the real owner. The former owner retained all the benefits of ownership without having title in his name. The trustee dealt with the public as if he were the true owner. Only the titled owner (trustee) and the true owner (beneficiary) knew of the arrangement.

The Mechanics of a Land Trust

As we discovered earlier, the land trust arrangement requires two legal documents:

1. A deed from the settlor to the trustee

2. A trust agreement between the settlor and the trustee that explains the details of the rights, powers, duties, and obligations of the parties

The trustee should be someone who is knowledgeable in real estate and financial matters. The trustee will remain in his or her position even on your death, so choose your trustee wisely!

The trust arrangement requires transferring title to your property to the trustee. A new deed will be recorded in the name of the trustee. All title to real estate will be removed from your name. A search of the real estate records will reveal that you own nothing. However, even if an attorney suspected that you had some interest in the trust, the public records would not reveal this information. The trust agreement is not recorded, only the deed. The trust agreement is a private arrangement between the beneficiary and the trustee. The identity of the beneficiary is not permitted to be revealed by the trustee. Generally, the assets of the parties to a lawsuit are not discoverable before a judgment is rendered. Before a lawsuit is commenced, it is nearly impossible for an attorney to find the identity of the beneficiary of the trust.

It is possible to conduct a detailed (and expensive) search of real estate records to determine if you used to own the property and have retitled the property in trust. However, the attorney will have to decide whether it is worth the risk of taking on the case, only to find out later that the trust may not be connected with you. Even if the attorney gets a judgment and discovers you are the beneficiary of the trust, he or she still has to take the additional steps of going to court and asking the judge to set aside the trust. Every "hoop" a creditor and his or her attorney are required to jump through costs them time and money.

Many people with whom I discuss land trusts fail to set up this device, because their attorney, Realtor, or accountant never heard of such a thing. Where I come from, it was impossible to sneak kids into a drive-in movie by hiding them in the trunk of your car, because everybody knew that trick! In other parts of the country, that stunt worked every day of the week. Likewise, if attorneys where you live don't know about land trusts, they also don't know how to get through them!

Legal and Tax Implications

A few final points on land trusts: First, there are no federal income tax consequences for transferring property into a land trust. The Internal Revenue Code requires that you continue to report the property as though it were owned outright in the beneficiary's name (IRC Sections 671–678). The land trust will not affect capital gains treatment, mortgage interest deduction, or depreciation rules.

You should be aware that a land trust is not a corporation and will not shield the beneficiary from liability. If someone slips and falls on the property, the beneficiary can be held liable. Thus, it may be a good idea to have the beneficiary of the trust be a corporation or other limited liability entity. This transfer can be accomplished easily and quietly by the beneficiary transferring his or her "beneficial interest" (similar to the transfer of shares of stock in a corporation). Keep in mind that such a transfer does not appear on the public records! (For an in-depth discussion on creating and using land trusts, I suggest my land trust home study course, *Step-by-Step Guide to Land Trusts*. Call 800-655-3632 for special discounts available to you as a purchaser of this book.)

Personal Property Trusts

A personal property trust (PPT) is a nominee-type trust, similar to a land trust. It can be used to hold title to any personal assets that are publicly held, such as an automobile, boat, bank account, or mortgage. A PPT can also be used to own your interest in a corporation or limited liability company.

CHAPTER 5

More Strategies for Appearing Broke

Mortgage Your Real Estate beyond Its Value

Having no assets avoids lawsuits, but being in debt works even better! A majority of middle-class America is in debt. You should make it appear that your assets are leveraged for more than their value, so creditors won't bother suing you. See Figure 5.1.

Mortgage Liens

Generally, there are two types of loans, unsecured and secured. An *unsecured loan* is called a "signature" loan; the lender will lend you money based on your credit and income. A typical unsecured loan is a credit card account. A *secured loan* is based on the value of the assets you intend to pledge as collateral. In some secured transactions (e.g., a car loan), the lender will hold title to your asset as collateral. In most transactions, the lender will request a security agreement (e.g., a mortgage or deed of trust) that will be filed in the county in which the asset sits.

FIGURE 5.1 Leverage Your Assets for More Than Their Value

Let's suppose that you had a house worth $100,000 with a first mortgage for $65,000. The property has $35,000 in equity. If you wanted to borrow $25,000 from a bank, the bank would require that you sign a promissory note and a mortgage for $25,000. The mortgage is a legal document in which you pledge your property as collateral for the loan (called a *deed of trust* in some states). If you default on a second mortgage loan, the lender will foreclose the property. Of course, the lender's mortgage is subordinate to the first mortgage on the property. In order for the bank to get its money back, it would have to foreclose the property, pay off the $65,000 first mortgage, and sell the property to recoup its money.

If you had a first and second mortgage on the property, a judgment creditor would have little recourse. The creditor would have to file the judgment lien, force the sale of your property, and pay off the first *and* second mortgages. In theory, it could get some money from the remaining proceeds.

The reality is that properties don't normally sell for their full market value at auction. Thus, even a property with 10 percent equity is not necessarily appealing to a party contemplating suing you.

Bank Line of Credit

If you have a lot of equity in your home, consider a bank line of credit. A line of credit (LOC) is an agreement by a lender to extend credit up to a certain amount for a certain time. It is similar to a credit card, in that you only pay interest on what you borrow. The lender gives you a checkbook, which allows you to activate the line of credit by writing a check. If you don't write any checks, the line of credit is not activated. An LOC is usually secured by a mortgage lien on your personal residence.

Let's say, for example, you own a home worth $300,000. You have a first mortgage for $200,000, leaving $100,000 equity for a creditor to attach. If you obtained a bank LOC for $100,000, a creditor would be third in line. On public record, the bank has a mortgage for $100,000 on the property. However, the creditor does not know if you have borrowed $1 or $100,000 on the bank LOC.

Creating Your Own Liens

Let's say you had equity in a property but didn't want to actually borrow money. An ideal situation would be for your close friend, relative, or corporation controlled by you to loan you money. You sign a mortgage, pledging your property as security for the loan or line of credit. To the outside world, it would appear that your property is "mortgaged to the hilt." The only document on public record is a mortgage showing a principal balance. If you paid back all of the debt but $100, the lien would still be valid, but the amount you still owed would not be public record (remember, the promissory note is not recorded, only the mortgage). The $100 balance due on the mortgage may not defeat a judgment creditor's position, but it will certainly deter a creditor considering the possibility of suing you.

Encumber Your Personal and Business Assets

Your personal property and business equipment can be mortgaged as well as your real estate. Typically, when you lease or purchase business equipment, the lender or supplier "perfects" his interest by filing a Form UCC-1 with the state and county recorder's office. The filing of the form gives the world notice that the lender has a lien on all property listed (a UCC-1 is the personal property equivalent of a mortgage; see the sample form in the Appendix). You could use this strategy effectively by having your "Uncle Ralph" lend you $10,000, secured by all of your personal and business assets (of course, you pay most of it back). If you own your automobile outright, you can amend the title at the Department of Motor Vehicles to reflect a secured lender, your Uncle Ralph.

Keep in mind that these "tricks" may not withstand a creditor's challenge, but they will deter many creditors whose claims may not be worth pursuing in court. Many people file lawsuits for "nuisance value" with the hope that you would rather pay to make it go away than pay a lawyer to defend you. These techniques may not deter the most tenacious creditors, but they will "separate the men from the boys," so to speak.

Keep in mind that it may be considered a criminal act in your state to file a document in a public place that is false. Do not simply file a mortgage, UCC-1, or lien that refers to an obligation that does not in fact exist.

"Devalue" Your Real Property

Besides encumbering your real estate financially, you can encumber it physically. Defects in the title to your property make it less valuable to a potential creditor.

One such strategy is to grant an easement to a friend or trusted relative. An *easement* is a right-of-way. If you search the real estate records in your county, you will find that many properties have easements for driveways, utility lines, pipes, etc. What if your best friend paid you $500 for an easement through the middle of your property? He or she would technically have the right to bulldoze your house!

Another such interest is a profit. A *profit* is the right to go onto the land of another and take something from the land, such as oil, water, minerals, etc. If someone has the right to come onto your land and take your trees, bushes, and grass, it will seriously affect the value of your property (or so it may appear to prying eyes).

Of course, you should keep a quitclaim deed in your filing cabinet in case you have a falling out with the friend or relative to whom you granted such an interest. This quitclaim deed will allow you to remove the encumbrance in a hurry if you need to clear the title to sell or refinance the property.

Convert "Nonexempt" Property to "Exempt" Property

Most creditors and collection attorneys know that certain property is exempt under federal and state laws from creditors' claims. You should be aware of what property is exempt from these claims and convert as much of your wealth as possible into exempt property (and do it now to avoid the pitfalls of fraudulent transfer laws). Having most of your wealth in the form of exempt property is as good as being broke!

Homestead Protection

In most states, the equity in your primary residence is exempt from creditors' claims. Only a few states provide an unlimited exception, so make certain that your equity remains about that amount. For example, if your state homestead protection is $25,000, a creditor cannot force the sale of your home if you have less than $25,000 in equity. (You may try using the strategies suggested above to reduce the market value of your home to effectively increase your homestead protection!) If you like golf and warm weather, consider moving to Florida, a state with unlimited homestead protection!

In some states, you must file a public document to "claim your homestead." Contact your local county recording office to find out the specific process as well as any exceptions to the protection in your state. You will find a summary of state homestead laws in the Appendix.

Wages

Believe it or not, most of your wages are exempt from execution by a creditor. The amount a creditor can "garnish" changes from state to state but usually does not exceed 25 percent (in most states, the exemption is not as generous for child support obligations). If you are self-employed and your state law exempts most of your wages from creditors' claims, give yourself a raise!

Life Insurance

In most states, both the cash value of an insurance policy and the proceeds are protected from creditors. The amount of protection changes from state to state, so check your local law.

Note on Life Insurance Trusts

A major blunder that most people make in estate planning is owning a life insurance policy. Few people realize that insurance proceeds are part of your taxable estate. If you have a $1,000,000 policy and $1,000,000 or more in other assets, your estate could be liable for several hundred thousand dollars in estate taxes! The solution to this problem is to set up an irrevocable life insurance trust, which owns the policy. When you die, the trust and not your estate is funded with the insurance proceeds. The trustee will be directed how to distribute the proceeds under the trust agreement. You can ask a lawyer to draft an irrevocable life insurance trust, although many insurance companies from which you buy the policy will set it up for a small fee.

Retirement Plans

Generally speaking, ERISA-qualified retirement plans, including 401(k)s, and pensions are protected from the claims of creditors (ERISA is a federal law governing employee benefit plans). IRAs, SEPs, and Keogh plans are generally not afforded the same protection. The amount of protection changes from state to state, so check your local law (a summary of state law protections of IRAs can be found on the Internet at <www.ici.org/issues/99_state_ira_bnkrptcy.html>).

Keep in mind that the Internal Revenue Service is a federal agency, and its power is therefore not limited by state law exemptions. In addition, most states have now eroded these protections when child support obligations are involved.

Fractionalize Your Ownership

Owning *part* of an asset can make it more difficult for a creditor to attach and sell it. For example, if you own a 40 percent interest in a family company, a creditor will have a difficult time reselling it. After all, who wants to be a minority-interest owner of a business with people he or she doesn't know (and who will certainly be hostile to him or her)?

Fractionalizing your ownership can also cause troubles. If your co-owners have legal problems, those problems can become yours; for example, if your co-owner is a spouse who doesn't work and has little risk of financial liability, this strategy can be effective.

SECTION THREE

Control, Don't Own!

CHAPTER 6

A Comparison of Business Entities

As we discussed in the Introduction, the best way to keep what you have is not to have anything in your name. You cannot lose what you do not own. In Section Three, we will discuss the different entities available to limit your exposure and spread your ownership. We will start with a review of the different entities available.

Sole Proprietorship

A *sole proprietorship* is just "you doing business." There is no filing requirement and no formal paperwork, unless you do business under a fictitious or trade name. In that case, you must usually file a "d/b/a" (doing business as) with the county or secretary of state in the state in which you do business.

As a sole proprietor, you report your income on Schedule C of your federal income tax return. Your liability is unlimited, because you and your business are one and the same. If your business is sued, your personal assets, your residence, and your money are at risk. If your business is bankrupt, you must file personal bankruptcy to avoid the business debts.

General Partnership

A *general partnership* is formed when two or more individuals or entities agree to carry on business together for a profit. No written partnership agreement is required, although it can be done that way. A general partnership can be created even if you did not intend it (i.e., a judge will let you know when you are sued for something someone else did on your behalf, sometimes known as "partnership by estoppel").

The partnership itself does not pay taxes; it files an informational tax return with the IRS. This return (IRS Form 1065) simply summarizes the income, expenses, profits, and losses of the partnership business. The bottom-line profit or loss "flows through" to the partners, who report their share of income or loss on Schedule E of their personal income tax returns (the partnership will send each of the partners an IRS Form K-1, which states the partner's share of profit or loss).

A general partnership does not afford liability protection for its partners. Partners are jointly and severally liable for each other's *tortious* (wrongful) acts. "Jointly" means that if one partner causes the partnership to be sued, all partners are liable; "severally" means that all partners are liable for 100 percent of the judgment. This means that if you are the "silent" partner who puts up and has the most money, you have the most to lose.

Limited Liability Partnership

Many states have enacted a new creature called a *limited liability partnership,* or LLP. The LLP is much like a general partnership, except it must be formally created by registering with the state (such registration is usually accomplished by simply filing a document and paying a fee). An existing general partnership can usually become an LLP by registering.

For tax purposes, the LLP is generally treated the same as a general partnership. The LLP files an information tax return, and the partners receive a K-1, from which they report their share of income or loss on their personal income tax return.

In some states, a registered LLP will protect all partners from ordinary debts of the partnership. In other states, the LLP is not a shield for all debts. In all states, the LLP will not protect the partners from their own tortious (wrongful) conduct. The LLP will, however, shield partners from liability for the tortious conduct of their partners. For example, an LLP comprised of lawyers and doctors may shield the partners from malpractice of their partners but not *their own* malpractice.

Corporations

A *corporation* is an entity that exists separate and apart from its shareholders. It requires the filing of a certificate with your secretary of state called an "articles of incorporation." The corporation issues stock to its owners called "shareholders." The shareholders elect a board of directors. The board of directors, in turn, appoints officers, such as president, secretary, and treasurer. See Figure 6.1.

The major policy decisions of a corporation are made by the board of directors in the form of a "resolution." The day-to-day functions of the corporation are performed by the officers of the company. The shareholders own the corporation but cannot directly run the corporation's business.

In most states, one individual can be the shareholder, director, and all of the officers. (In a few states, the offices of president and secretary cannot be held by the same person—check your state law.) Thus, a one-man corporation is perfectly legal, but the individual must be careful to disclose the capacity in which he or she is acting (president, chairman of the board, etc.).

FIGURE 6.1 Corporation Hierarchy

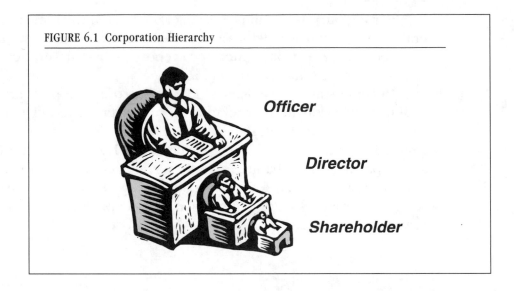

Officer

Director

Shareholder

The S Corporation versus the C Corporation

There are basically two types of corporations for tax purposes: C corporations and S corporations. A corporation is a C corporation by default; the S status must be elected.

All large, publicly traded corporations (e.g., IBM) are C corporations. A C corporation files its own tax return (IRS Form 1120) and pays taxes on its income. The good news is, the tax rates for regular corporations are usually lower than personal tax rates up to about $100,000. The bad news is that when profits are distributed, they are taxed again on the shareholders' personal income tax returns. This is what we commonly call "double taxation." However, C corporations can permit employees to take certain "fringe benefits," such as health plans, medical reimbursements, and life insurance. None of these benefits are taxable to the employee, and the expense is deductible to the corporation. As you can see, a C corporation can be a great tax savings vehicle for small family businesses.

An S corporation is a "flow-through" entity. It files an informational return (IRS Form 1120-S) and profits and losses flow through to the shareholders. An S corporation, like a partnership, sends each of its shareholders an IRS Form K-1, which states the shareholder's share of profit or loss. This profit is not normally subject to self-employment tax. Unlike a C corporation, the S corporation does not have the same fringe benefits, but it still has tax advantages over a sole proprietorship (namely, limitation of self-employment tax).

Liability of Shareholders

In the absence of special circumstances, a corporation's shareholders are not personally liable to third parties for debts or wrongful conduct. However, if an individual shareholder is sued for events unrelated to the corporation's business, the creditor can attach the shareholder's interest in the corporation and take control of the corporation's assets (if the shares represent a majority voting interest in the corporation). While a corporation is an excellent device for liability protection from the creditors of the corporation, it is not the best device for merely holding assets (because a creditor can seize the debtor's stock certificates and take control of the corporation through the "back door").

If the corporation is sued, there are some circumstances where the court may permit a litigant to "pierce the corporate veil" and go directly against the shareholders. (In some states, officers, directors, and any other person or entity in direct control of the corporation may also be held personally liable.) Usually, a court will not permit a plaintiff to seek redress against a shareholder, officer, or director unless it appears that the corporation is a "sham." The plaintiff must prove that the corporation is not separate from its shareholders but merely an instrumentality for the wrongdoing of the shareholders. This is why it is critical that you follow all corporate formalities, especially if you are a one-person corporation. The most common situation in which a court will permit a litigant to pierce the corporate veil is where the corporate formalities are not present.

These corporate formalities are not very cumbersome and will save you from disaster if you are sued or audited by the IRS. (Visit <www.legalwiz.com> for information on do-it-yourself kits for setting up and operating your own corporation and creating a "bulletproof" paper trail.)

Trusts

We discussed the land trust in Section Two as an asset protection device. In reality, the land trust is more of an "asset-hiding" device. If a creditor knew that you were the beneficiary of a land trust, the creditor could attach your beneficial interest. This is because a land trust is a revocable living trust, and such trusts do not protect the beneficiary's interest from the claims of his or her creditors. (The theory is that because the beneficiary has unlimited access to the trust assets while he or she is still alive, so should his or her creditors.)

Revocable Trusts

While a revocable living trust does not have an asset protection feature, it does still have a purpose in estate planning. The typical living trust (also called a "loving trust" by financial companies) initially is set up with the grantor, trustee, and beneficiary being the same person. The living trust will provide that on the death of the grantor a successor trustee be appointed to manage or distribute trust assets to successor beneficiaries. So long as the grantor is living, he or she can revoke the trust and retitle the assets.

Once the grantor of the living trust dies, the trust becomes irrevocable and takes on a new life as a truly separate legal entity. Any property owned by the trust is not subject to probate, because it is not owned by the grantor or his or her estate. A living trust will usually provide that if the successor beneficiaries are still minors, the assets will be held and managed by the trustee until the beneficiaries reach a certain age. Alternatively, the trust may provide that the assets be distributed at the death of the grantor. The trust document can be drafted any number of ways to meet the desires of the grantor. You can even create a trust for a pet!

The A-B Trust

The "A-B" or credit shelter trust is created by married couples (see Figure 6.2). Because transfers to a spouse on death are exempt from estate tax, the grantor creates a trust that splits into two trusts on his or her death. One trust is revocable (the "A" trust), the other irrevocable (the "B" trust). The "B" trust provides for income for the surviving spouse for his or her life. Additionally, the trustee of the "B" trust can distribute the corpus of the trust to the extent necessary for the surviving spouse's health, support, and maintenance. The balance of the "B" trust corpus is distributed to other heirs on the death of the surviving spouse without estate tax.

The "A" trust is a simple, revocable living trust for the surviving spouse, who can amend or revoke the "A" trust at any time as he or she sees fit. The assets in the "A" trust become part of his or her taxable estate.

Probate Estate versus Taxable Estate

There is a difference between a person's *taxable* estate and his or her *probate* estate. As discussed earlier, a probate estate consists of the assets held in title by the decedent on death. These assets must go through the state probate court process before they are distributed to heirs. A person's *taxable* estate is the amount of assets that are subject to federal income tax. Assets held in a revocable living trust are still "owned" by the decedent; thus, while a living trust may avoid a state court probate proceeding, it will not necessarily avoid federal estate tax.

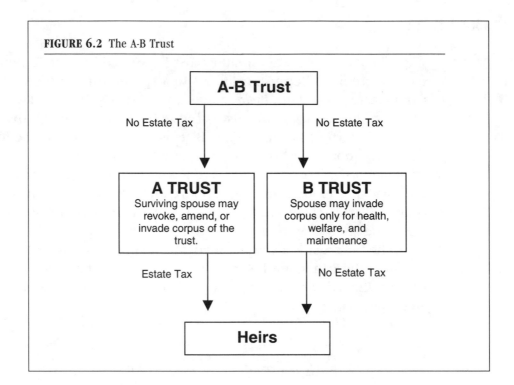

FIGURE 6.2 The A-B Trust

Irrevocable Trust

An irrevocable trust can provide very good asset protection. With proper planning, an irrevocable trust can insulate your assets from claims of outside parties. The operating principle is that the trust—a separate entity from you—now owns the assets. If the trust contains a "spendthrift" provision, the trustee has authority to withhold distributions of income and principal. To the extent the trustee can withhold income from you, he or she can also withhold it from your creditors. Revocable trusts allow you to have complete access to your assets, which is why creditors can also go after the same assets.

In most states, you cannot be the trustee or beneficiary of the trust if you want to completely protect the trust assets from the claims of creditors. Alaska, Delaware, and Nevada have recently enacted "self-settled" creditor-protection trust laws, but the waters are largely untested for these trusts. And unless you live in the state where the trust was formed, it is unlikely a judge will allow you to protect your assets from creditors using these trusts. Siblings or in-laws are a good choice for trustees, because they are beyond your legal control, yet hopefully are looking out for your best interests.

Keep in mind that these types of trusts are irrevocable; that is, once you place the assets into trust, you cannot get them back. Typically, these types of trusts are created primarily for estate planning, so you may wish to forgo using them if you are under the age of 40. Even beyond that age, you may choose to use an irrevocable trust for select items of property, such as your residence (known as a "qualified personal residence trust," or QPRT) or your life insurance policy (known as an "irrevocable life insurance trust").

Note on the QPRT

The QPRT (qualified personal residence trust) can be an effective estate planning technique for someone with an expensive home in a rapidly appreciating market. The QPRT works as follows: The owner of a personal residence transfers the residence to a trust, retaining the right to live in the residence for a specified period of years. At the end of that period of years, the trust is terminated and the children of the grantor (or other designated beneficiaries) become the owners of the residence. At the termination of the trust, the residence is no longer part of the grantor's taxable estate.

During the term of the trust, the grantor is treated as the taxable owner of the property. Thus, the grantor can take advantage of the mortgage interest deduction. The property can be sold without capital gains (exempt up to $250,000 of gain) and be replaced with another personal residence. Since the grantor is still the owner of the property for federal income tax purposes, the residence is included in his or her taxable estate if he or she dies before the termination of the trust.

If you do choose to create an irrevocable trust, make certain that you use an attorney and/or CPA who is well versed in estate planning, gift, and income tax law.

Offshore Trust

Certain countries offer excellent asset protection for trusts created and/or located in their jurisdictions. If you have a significant amount of "portable" wealth (cash, securities, diamonds), you may choose to set up a trust in an offshore jurisdiction.

The word *offshore* doesn't necessarily mean an island; any jurisdiction outside the United States (even Mexico) is considered offshore. The very fact that your wealth is located far away will hinder all but the most tenacious creditors. Such a creditor would have to hire an attorney who specializes in international law, and these attorneys charge far more than the average "ambulance chasers."

Another major reason people set up trusts in foreign jurisdictions is the favorable fraudulent conveyance laws. In the United States, fraudulent conveyance laws can be used to set aside a trust, even if there was no actual fraud when the property was transferred into trust. Just the fact that you *made* yourself broke and later incurred large debts can be sufficient evidence for a creditor to challenge a conveyance. In some states, the statute of limitations (the maximum period in which a creditor can challenge a fraudulent transfer) is seven years (discussed more in Chapter 10).

In many foreign jurisdictions, as long as there was no actual fraud on the creation of the trust, the creditor cannot challenge the transfer. In fact, the law is so loose that a creditor must prove that the transfer was fraudulent beyond a reasonable doubt! The statute of limitations for challenging a conveyance in some of these jurisdictions is only two years. In the United States, it takes almost that long to complete a lawsuit!

Many offshore jurisdictions will not enforce a judgment from an American court. The party must commence a brand-new lawsuit in the foreign jurisdiction. And here's the best part: Many of those jurisdictions do not permit attorneys to work on a contingent-fee basis!

Another reason why people like foreign-based trusts is the amount of control they can exercise over the trust assets. As stated above, a trust created in the United States leaves the grantor (the one who creates the trust) with little or no power over the trust assets. If the grantor is also the beneficiary of the trust or exerts some control over the trustee, most American courts will rule that a creditor can get to the trust assets.

The ruling is much different for assets based in foreign jurisdictions, where the law allows a person to create a trust for his or her own benefit and still protect the trust assets from creditors. This can present a dilemma, because a judge in an American court may order the grantor/beneficiary to remove the assets from the foreign trust to pay his creditors. Failure to do so could result in contempt of court. However, these trusts usually contain a "duress" clause, which permits the trustee of the foreign-based trust (who is not under the jurisdiction of the American court) to ignore such a demand. Thus, in theory, the grantor/beneficiary cannot be punished, because the trustee won't give him or her the money. This "theory," of course, may not hold water with an angry American judge, who may throw you in jail for failing to obey the order. Furthermore, if you try to file for bankruptcy protection, your petition for discharge of debts may be denied protection if the judge believes you are "hiding" assets offshore.

In light of recent terrorist activities, the U.S. government is keeping a close eye on offshore transactions. In addition, many jurisdictions that were once "secret" are starting to cooperate with the American government.

Keep in mind that the IRS has detailed reporting requirements for offshore assets. Your failure to report these assets could result in severe penalties. Furthermore, the expense of using offshore trusts may not be worthwhile, unless a substantial amount of capital is at risk and can be physically moved to the foreign jurisdiction. The concept of moving title to real estate into an offshore trust is often sold by trust promoters, but it is nonsense; an American judge can void such a transaction if the asset is located in his or her jurisdiction.

Business Trust

A *business trust* is an irrevocable trust used for liability and creditor protection. A board of trustees runs the trust business, similar to a corporation. The beneficiaries receive "certificates of ownership," similar to stock certificates in a corporation. For federal income tax purposes, a business trust is generally treated as a corporation. A business trust is also referred to as an *unincorporated business trust,* unincorporated business organization, and Massachusetts business trust.

Business trusts were once popular in Massachusetts (hence the name Massachusetts business trust), because there was a time when corporations could not own real estate. However, business trusts are not generally recommended because of nonuniformity of treatment from state to state. In some states, business trusts do not provide liability protection; in others, they do. Furthermore, the IRS has designated business trusts as being a possible "abusive" trust.

Abusive Trusts

A rash of scam artists has been promoting what is called a "pure trust," "pure equity trust," "common law trust," or "constitutional trust." The claim being made by the promoters of these trusts is that you can legally reduce your income and FICA tax by using these trusts. They cite U.S. Supreme Court cases for their legal position and actually appear to know what they are talking about.

The reality is, these trusts are a scam. The IRS Criminal Investigation Division has created a special task force to prosecute the promoters of these trusts. In addition, the IRS has labeled certain types of trusts as being "abusive" and automatically suspect. These trusts do *not* include land trusts and personal property trusts as described previously, which are not used for avoiding income taxes.

You can read more about abusive trusts in the IRS article on these trusts in the Appendix.

Limited Partnership

A *limited partnership* has at least one limited partner and one general partner. Most states require the filing of a certificate with the state in order to be recognized as a limited partnership.

The limited partners generally have no liability beyond their contribution to the partnership. If the limited partnership business fails, the creditors of the partnership cannot go after the limited partners for debts. Furthermore, limited partners are not personally liable for wrongful acts committed by the general partners. In exchange for this limited liability, the limited partners give up their right to participate in the control and management of the partnership.

The general partners run the management of the partnership. The general partners control the cash distributions to the partners. The general partners also have unlimited liability, as in a general partnership. Creditors of the partnership can look to the general partners' personal assets, if the limited partnership's assets are insufficient. Furthermore, the general partners are liable to third parties for wrongful conduct within the partnership business (e.g., a "slip-and-fall" lawsuit). Thus, a corporation is usually better for pure liability protection for its owners (and as you may have guessed, a general partner of a limited partner can also be a corporation).

The limited partnership does not pay federal income taxes. It files a partnership return of income (IRS Form 1065) and issues a Form K-1 to the partners. The partners report the partnership income or loss on their personal tax returns. The partners must pay income tax on all gains, whether or not the profit is distributed.

Creditors of individual partners cannot take a partner's place in the partnership. A creditor may garnish the partner's share of income (called a *charging order*), but has no right to participate in the management or utilize partnership property. The creditor is only entitled to attach the income that the partner is currently receiving. Thus, if a limited partner's income is "charged" by a creditor, the general partner can frustrate the creditor by not distributing income to the partners. Obviously, the general partner should be someone under the limited partner's control.

A Surprise for the Creditor from the IRS!

According to IRS Revenue Ruling 77-137, a creditor that charges the interest of a limited partner is the "owner" of such interest and *must report the distributive share of partnership items of income, gain or loss, deduction, and credit attributable to the assigned interest . . . in the same manner and the same amounts that would be required if [the assignee] was a substitute limited partner.* Thus, the creditor would be responsible for income tax liability on the partner's undistributed income!

Family Limited Partnership

Let's look at a variation known as a *family limited partnership* (FLP). The term *family* comes from a provision of the Internal Revenue Code that deals with the treatment of income shifted between family members. Generally speaking, an FLP is a limited partnership formed between family members.

Suppose that you and your spouse create a limited partnership to hold your family's liquid investment assets. Your limited partnership contributions are all of your stocks, cash, CDs, and mutual funds totaling $300,000. Your partnership agreement could state that your spouse will act as general partner with a 2 percent share (the size of

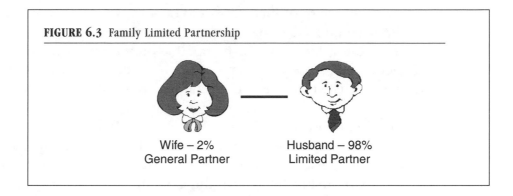

FIGURE 6.3 Family Limited Partnership

Wife – 2%
General Partner

Husband – 98%
Limited Partner

the general partnership share does not affect the general partner's power to manage the partnership's affairs). You agree in writing that your contributions constitute a 98 percent limited partnership interest. See Figure 6.3.

The partnership agreement could state further that the limited partnership shall have the right to buy out the general partner for his share of the partnership and appoint a new general partner to replace her. The "you" in this example is the husband; we are making the wife the general partner, because we assume that the husband's risk of getting sued is higher. If the opposite were true, then we would arrange the partnership accordingly.

Let's suppose that you are sued, and a creditor obtains a $50,000 judgment against your name. The creditor can attach your limited partnership interest, but only to the extent of your income as a limited partner (called a *charging order*). The creditor who attaches a limited partnership interest cannot participate in the management of the partnership and thus cannot force the general partner, your spouse, to distribute income. As general partner, your spouse stops paying the limited partner's distributions, because in his or her discretion the limited partnership would be better served to reinvest the capital.

One year later, the creditor still has a $50,000 unsatisfied judgment. To top it off, the partnership sends the creditor an IRS Form K-1 for the creditor's share of your "phantom" income. In our example, the partnership assets are worth $300,000. At 10 percent annual return, your share of income would be approximately $30,000—the creditor would have to pay income taxes in the ballpark of $10,000! If the creditor does not pay the tax due on your undistributed share of income, the IRS will come after the creditor. You will be in a strong position to force your creditor to settle the claim for a fraction of its value.

Let's suppose a creditor sues your spouse and tries to attack your spouse's general partnership interest. At that point, the partnership exercises its power under the partnership agreement to buy out her general partnership interest in the amount of $2,000, or 2 percent. The partnership then finds a new general partner. With proper planning, this may not be considered a "fraudulent" conveyance, because the general partner received full compensation for her partnership share. As you can see, the limited partnership is one of the few entities that affords control over your money, yet still provides you with asset protection.

Estate Planning

The FLP is an excellent estate planning and income tax reduction tool, if used properly. See Figure 6.4. Many estate planning professionals suggest that you gift small limited partnership shares to your children every year, so that the size of your taxable estate is reduced on your death ($11,000 worth per year or less, so that no gift tax is due). Control of the assets during your life is still retained by virtue of your spouse's general partnership interest. The value of your remaining interest is further reduced for estate tax purposes, because it is not a controlling interest. (After all, who would buy the share for full value on the open market?)

Limited Liability Company

Limited liability companies, or LLCs, are the newest breed of limited liability entities. LLCs are a creation of state law and are now recognized in all states. The LLC, like a corporation or limited

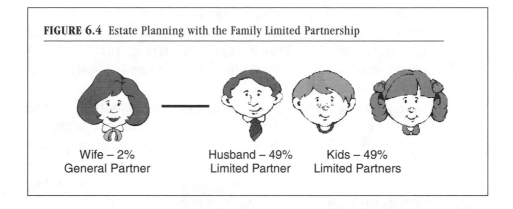

FIGURE 6.4 Estate Planning with the Family Limited Partnership

Wife – 2%
General Partner

Husband – 49%
Limited Partner

Kids – 49%
Limited Partners

partnership, requires filing an "articles of organization" with your secretary of state in order to be valid.

The LLC is owned by partners, which are called "members." As with a corporation, the members are not liable beyond their contributions to the company. Unlike a limited partnership, all members can participate in the management of the company without personal liability for company debts or lawsuits against the company.

The LLC can be run by its members or by a "manager," which can be a corporate entity or individual who may or may not be a member. When an LLC is manager managed (as opposed to member managed), it is similar in operation to a limited partnership. The manager makes all the day-to-day decisions, signs for appropriate obligations, and so on. However, the manager is not personally liable for company debts or lawsuits against the company (a general partner of a limited partnership has personal liability for obligations of the limited partnership). The members that are not also managers are simply passive investors, akin to limited partners of a limited partnership.

When an LLC is member managed, all of the members can participate in the management and control of the company. A member-managed LLC is thus very similar in operation to a general partnership, with one notable exception—the members are not liable for the debts or liabilities of the company.

By default, an LLC with two or more members is taxed as a partnership. The LLC files a partnership tax return (IRS Form 1065), and each member will receive an IRS Form K-1. Like a partnership, members can receive income and deductions in proportions that may or may not be equal to their ownership shares. Thus, the LLC is the only entity that offers the flexibility of a partnership with the protection of a corporation.

In most states, an LLC can be formed with just one member (called a "single-member" LLC). In this case, the company is disregarded for federal income tax purposes. For example, if a business is run as a sole proprietor and then changed to an LLC, the individual would have liability protection under state law but would continue to report on Schedule C of his or her federal income tax return.

In most states, a member's interest in an LLC cannot be attached by a creditor. Like a limited partnership interest, the creditor's remedy is generally limited to a charging order. Although the LLC may appear to be an excellent tool for asset protection, it has not been tested in court as extensively as corporations. The few court cases that have dealt with the issue thus far have applied the same tests for "piercing" that have been applied to corporations.

Important Note on Using FLPs and LLCs

If you use a limited partnership, FLP, or LLC to hold assets, you must have a valid business purpose for the liability protection to be enforceable. Thus, a limited partnership with your personal residence as its sole asset is not a valid business entity, unless you pay rent to the partnership.

If you consider an LLC, make certain you use an attorney and/or a CPA who is familiar with your state's law and relevant IRS rulings. Only time will tell whether the LLC will become the ultimate asset and wealth protection device.

(For information on do-it-yourself kits for creating and using limited partnerships and limited liability companies, visit my Web site at <www.legalwiz.com>.)

Summary of Legal and Tax Issues

There are four issues you'll want to consider when choosing your business structure:

1. How easy it is to create, run, and dissolve the organization

2. Tax savings and reporting requirements

3. The burden of yearly paperwork

4. Liability and asset protection

See Figure 6.5 for a comparison of business entities.

Formation Issues

As we discussed in Chapter 2, a sole proprietorship is just "you doing business." There is no filing requirement and no formal paperwork, except if you do business under a fictitious or trade name. Thus, a sole proprietorship is the easiest form of business to start and run.

As we discussed above, a general partnership is formed when two or more individuals or business entities agree to carry on business together for a profit. No formal written partnership agreement is required; a partnership can be made on a handshake.

A corporation, limited partnership, and limited liability company all require the filing of a certificate with your secretary of state.

FIGURE 6.5 Comparison Chart of Business Entities

Attribute	LLC	Sole Proprietorship	General Partnership	Limited Partnership	C Corporation	S Corporation	Irrevocable Trust
Lawsuit Protection	Yes	No	No	Yes (limited partners only)	Yes	Yes	Yes
Privacy	Some	No	No	Some	Some	Some	Yes
Creditor Protection	Yes	No	Some	Yes	Some	Some	Probably
Interest Easily Transferred	Yes	Maybe	Maybe	Maybe	Yes	Yes	Maybe
Requires Formalities	Some	No	No	Some	Yes	Yes	Some
Ease of Creation	Somewhat	Yes	Yes	Somewhat	No	No	No
Requires Separate Return	Yes (informational only)	No	Yes (informational only)	Yes (informational only)	Yes	Yes (informational only)	Yes
Employee Benefits	Some	Few	Some	Some	Yes	Some	No
Minimum People Required	1 (most states)	1	2	2	1	1	NA

Tax Implications

As a sole proprietor, you report income, expenses, profits, and losses on Schedule C of your federal income tax return. Your profit is subject to personal income tax rates, whether or not the money is siphoned out or reinvested in the business. Your Schedule C income is also subject to self-employment tax of 12.4 percent up to the taxable limit of Social Security (about $87,000) and 2.9 percent Medicare tax on all income earned. (The good news is that you receive a deduction on your federal income tax return for one-half of the self-employment tax.)

A partnership (general or limited) itself does not pay taxes; it files an informational tax return with the IRS. This return (IRS Form 1065) simply summarizes the income, expenses, profits, and losses of the partnership's business. The bottom-line profit or loss "flows through" to the partners, who report their share of income or loss on Schedule E of their personal income tax returns. (The partnership will send each of the partners an IRS Form K-1, which states the partner's share of profit or loss.) This profit is subject to personal income tax rates, whether or not the money is distributed or reinvested. This income is generally subject to self-employment tax.

A partnership may, in certain circumstances, permit its owners to allocate profits and losses in a manner inconsistent with their share of ownership. For example, a partner who puts up a significant amount of cash may insist on taking a greater share of the profit.

For tax purposes, the IRS has elected to treat a limited liability company the same as a partnership, so long as there are at least two members. A single-member LLC is "disregarded" for income tax purposes (the members of the LLC report the income and loss on their personal returns).

An S corporation is treated similarly to a partnership in that it has pass-through treatment of profits and losses. Also, shareholder distributions are not generally subject to self-employment tax.

A C corporation can be a tax nightmare or a bonus, depending on how it is used. If you want to retain profits inside the C corporation for later investment, you can reduce your overall income tax liability. In addition, if you pay for your own health insurance and medical costs with after-tax dollars, the C corporation can allow you 100 percent deduction for these items. There is no one-size-fits-all, so review your personal situation with your tax advisor.

Besides liability protection, the corporation will provide audit protection. Statistically speaking, your chances of being audited as a sole proprietor are about three times greater than your chances of being audited as a corporation. This only applies for small businesses reporting less than $100,000 of income. The IRS knows that corporations have very little assets at this level of income, and that the shareholders are probably siphoning off the income every year. Thus, an audit of the corporation will not yield the IRS any assets to seize.

Annual Paperwork

All of the entities discussed above require federal income tax filings. The corporation (C or S) requires the most amount of annual paperwork in the form of shareholder and director meetings. The paperwork is not cumbersome compared to the benefits a corporation can offer.

Liability Issues

Your liability as a sole proprietor is unlimited, because you and your business are one and the same. If your business is sued, your personal assets, your residence, and your money are at risk. If your business goes bust, you must file for personal bankruptcy protection to avoid the business debts.

A general partnership affords no liability protection for its partners. Partners are jointly and severally liable for each other's tortious acts (e.g., auto accident, "slip and fall," etc.). "Jointly" means that if one partner causes the partnership to be sued, all partners are liable; "severally" means that all partners are liable for 100 percent of the judgment. This means that if you are the silent partner who puts up and has the most money, you have the most to lose. Even if you are a 5 percent partner and do nothing wrong, you can still be held 100 percent accountable for the acts of your partners. While a general partnership is a simple and popular form of doing business, it can be hazardous to your financial health.

A limited partnership affords liability protection for the limited partners only. The general partners have unlimited liability. In most cases, a corporation should be used as a general partner for a limited partnership.

Both the corporation and LLC offer complete liability protection for the owners of the company. Thus, the use of an LLC versus a corporation becomes more of a tax issue than a liability issue. From an asset protection standpoint, the LLC is more effective for accumulating assets, because a creditor's remedy is limited to a charging order. The ownership of stock in a corporation is not similarly protected from creditor attachment.

CHAPTER 7

Putting the Pieces Together

Separate Assets According to Risk

A wise investor always spreads out his or her risk. Diversification applies to asset protection as well. The more you spread out the ownership of your assets, the less a creditor can take from you. By spreading the ownership of assets over various entities, you reduce the risk of loss to whatever each entity owns.

Safe versus Risk Assets

Separate your "safe" assets from your "risk" assets. Safe assets do not create liability by virtue of their ownership. Examples of safe assets are:

- Cash, savings, and checking accounts

- Stocks, bonds, CDs, and mutual funds

- Personal residence (somewhat, depending on how many kids are in the neighborhood, whether you have a pool, etc.)

The limited partnership and the limited liability company are good for holding safe assets, because the assets themselves do not create a risk of liability. Keep in mind that the general partners of a limited partnership are still exposed to tort liability arising from the limited partnership business. In the example of the family limited partnership in the last chapter, the creditor came after one of the partners for a judgment unrelated to the partnership business. Thus, a limited partnership is not the best device for holding a high-risk business or rental property. Such assets may be more appropriate for a corporation or limited liability company.

"Risk" assets create liability simply because you own them. Examples of risk assets are:

- Professional practices (lawyer, CPA, doctor, dentist, etc.)

- Rental properties

- Boats, planes, automobiles (especially when driven by teenagers)

- Restaurant, bar, or hotel

- Any business with employees or dangerous assets

Since "risk" assets create the risk of lawsuits against you personally, you may consider using a corporation or limited liability company to hold the assets. You can reduce your risk further by placing your risk assets into separate limited liability entities. A famous court case involved a New York cab company that created a separate corporation for each of its automobiles.

FIGURE 7.1 Splitting Up Business Assets

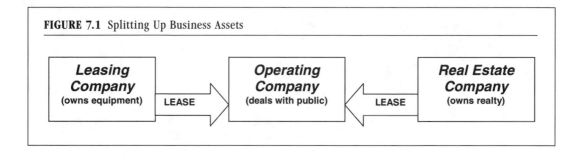

Separate Personal Assets from Business Assets—and Business Assets from Your Business

As discussed earlier, never do business as a sole proprietor—if your business is sued, your personal assets are at risk. Some people are smart enough to use a corporation or LLC to separate their business assets from their personal assets, but then make the mistake of having their business buy significant assets (e.g., automobiles, office buildings, equipment, etc.). If the business is sued, the creditor of the business can go after the automobiles, office buildings, and equipment.

One strategy is to divide the business into two or more parts. One entity would own relatively few assets and perform the risky part of the business. Another entity would own most of the assets and lease them to the former entity. A third entity, such as a family limited partnership, could own the real estate or office building. See Figure 7.1.

Keep in mind that these entities must be carefully maintained and deal at arm's length to avoid a court labeling one as the "alter ego" of the other. In addition, make sure your tax advisor is mindful of the "sibling" tax issue (Section 482 of the Internal Revenue Code allows the IRS to "lump together" affiliated corporations for income tax purposes).

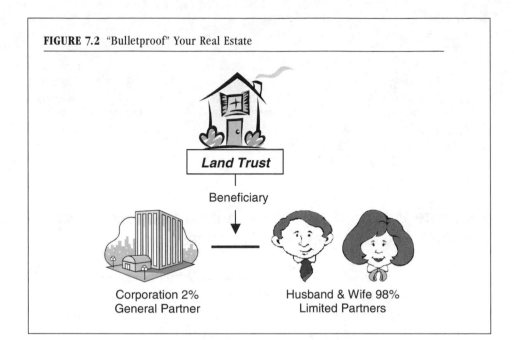

FIGURE 7.2 "Bulletproof" Your Real Estate

Land Trust

Beneficiary

Corporation 2%
General Partner

Husband & Wife 98%
Limited Partners

Combine Entities for Virtually "Bulletproof" Protection of Your Real Estate

An excellent way to ensure lawsuit protection of your real estate is to combine a land trust with a limited partnership and a corporation (see Figure 7.2). As discussed earlier, the limited partner's interest in a limited partnership is virtually "untouchable." Although in control of the partnership, a general partner is subjected to personal liability. What you need is a general partner under your control to "stand in" and take the hit.

The solution for virtually "bulletproof" protection is to have a corporation be the general partner of a limited partnership. The corporation only needs to have a small interest for the purposes of control. If the limited partnership were sued, the general partner and not the limited partners would be liable. If the corporation had little or no assets, the limited partners could "cut it loose" by buying out its share for a token amount. The limited partners would then have a new corporation become the general partner.

Now let's add one more layer of protection for holding real estate: the real estate is titled in a land trust. The beneficiary of the land trust would be the limited partnership, with a corporation as a 2 percent general partner. The corporation, of course, should be under ownership or control of the limited partners (i.e., the limited partners could also be the stockholders of the corporation).

Variation: The Limited Liability Company

In the above scenario, you may consider an LLC instead of a corporation/limited partnership combination. It involves less paperwork than using two entities. Some states, such as California and Texas, impose a high annual franchise tax on the use of LLCs, which makes using multiple limited partnerships more cost effective. In high franchise tax states, it is cheaper to use multiple limited partnerships than multiple LLCs.

Here Comes the Lawsuit

Continuing with the above scenario, let's suppose a tenant decides to sue the owner of the property. The first layer of protection is the land trust. Even if the tenant or his or her attorney knew what a land trust was, they would have to figure out who the beneficiary was. The attorney would then have to ask a court to set aside the land trust.

Even if the attorney were able to get that far, he or she would come across a limited partnership (or an LLC). The attorney could try to sue the general partner, only to find that it was a corporation. If he or she obtained a judgment against the corporation, its only asset would be a 2 percent share of the limited partnership. The limited partners then decide to cut the general partner loose by buying out its 2 percent share. The attorney could then try to sue the limited partner, which would be futile. In a last desperate attempt, the attorney tries to persuade the court that the corporate general partner is a sham and should be pierced. The court agrees and a judgment is entered against your name. By the time this whole process is complete, the rest of your cash is safe in other LLCs and trusts.

The more roadblocks you put in front of potential creditors, the less likely they will sue you. If they insist on suing you anyway, you will be able to stall their collection efforts for years and force them to settle their claim for a fraction of its value.

Multiple Corporations for Maximum Protection

Using your home state corporation and a Nevada corporation, you can use multiple corporations to encumber and separate assets. (See Figure 7.3.) The plan is a four-step process.

Step 1. Create a Corporation in Your Home State

Make certain that this corporation has a physical address in your home state and follows the proper corporate formalities outlined in this book.

Step 2. Create a Second Corporation in Nevada

Make certain that this corporation has a physical address in Nevada and follows the proper corporate formalities outlined in this book. It is best that the Nevada corporation not have the same shareholders, directors, and officers.

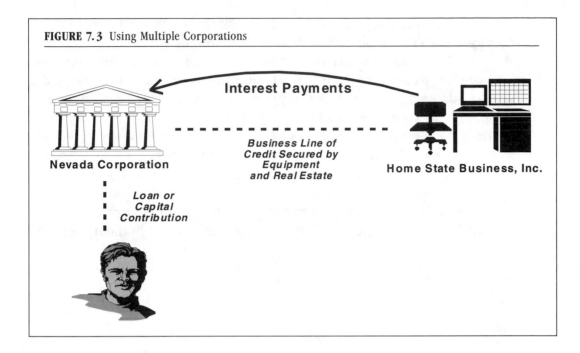

FIGURE 7.3 Using Multiple Corporations

Interest Payments

Nevada Corporation

*Business Line of
Credit Secured by
Equipment
and Real Estate*

Home State Business, Inc.

*Loan or
Capital
Contribution*

Step 3. "Fund" the Nevada Corporation with Capital

Funding can be accomplished by the purchase of stock or by you lending money to the corporation. Either way, make certain that there is a legal and legitimate paper trail. Execute a promissory note if you lend money and make sure you receive interest. It must look like any normal loan between you and a third-party corporation.

Step 4. Have the Nevada Corporation Lend Money to the Home State Corporation

Have the Nevada corporation send your home state corporation a letter of solicitation advertising for loans. Fill out a loan application and send it back to the Nevada corporation. Have the Nevada corporation send back a letter of approval and a promissory note to execute. Execute the note and send it back to the Nevada corporation, along with the appropriate security instruments.

Here's another variation: Instead of lending money from one corporation to another, simply lease equipment or real estate. Have the Nevada corporation own the plant, factory, and/or real estate and lease it to your home state corporation. If there are no such assets, have the Nevada corporation charge your home state corporation for marketing or business consultation services. As you can see, there are many creative variations to the formula. Just make certain that there is a legitimate consideration for the payments and that the Nevada corporation deals at arm's length with your home state corporation. You can find a sample Nevada Corporations filing packet in the Appendix.

CHAPTER 8

Sample Asset Protection Plans

In this chapter, we will explore sample asset protection plans based on different scenarios. Keep in mind that there is no one-size-fits-all formula. In addition to the tax and estate planning issues, you need to include the reality factor; that is, you need to determine what level of protection you need and what level of paperwork and mechanics you feel comfortable with. The more layers you build, the more protection you gain, but the more difficult your life becomes.

The Real Estate Entrepreneur

Let's look at Larry Landlord's picture. Larry owns three rental properties. Larry is married with no children. Larry places title to each property in a separate land trust, making a limited liability company the beneficiary of all three trusts. He and his wife are the members of the LLC. See Figure 8.1.

If Larry is sued on a matter unrelated to the real estate business, a creditor can only seek a "charging" against Larry's interest in the LLC. The LLC's operating agreement states that distributions of

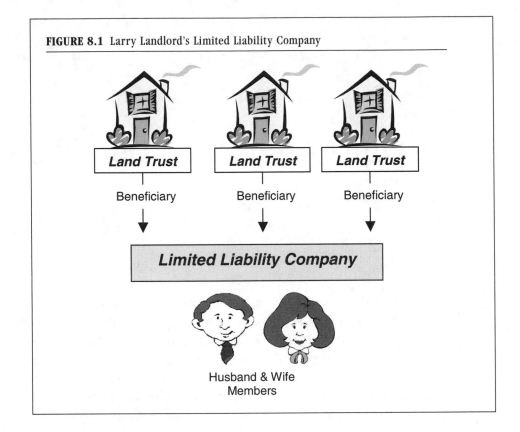

FIGURE 8.1 Larry Landlord's Limited Liability Company

income require a unanimous vote of the members. Larry's wife, of course, will never agree to a distribution if it means losing that income to a creditor. Thus, Larry will have good asset protection.

From a lawsuit protection standpoint, a suit by a tenant in one of the properties could be limited by the land trust that owns title. However, a smart attorney (say, 1 in 150) would know that the beneficiary of a land trust is liable for mishaps on the property. Thus, the LLC would be liable, which means the LLC could potentially lose everything it owns (to wit: the other properties). However, a court judgment against the LLC would have no bearing on Larry's personal assets.

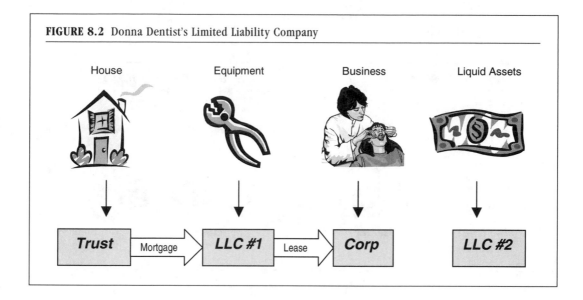

FIGURE 8.2 Donna Dentist's Limited Liability Company

The Single Professional

Let's look at Donna Dentist's picture. Donna, a single professional, operates a dental practice as a sole proprietor. She owns $150,000 worth of business equipment and employs four people. She also has a $500,000 home with 50 percent equity and $500,000 invested in the stock market.

Donna should incorporate her dental practice. Although she cannot protect herself from her own malpractice, she can protect herself from the liabilities of her employees. In addition, Donna should form a second company, such as an LLC, to own the business assets. The LLC could lease the equipment back to her operating company. Finally, Donna should form another LLC to hold her liquid assets, namely the stocks. As a smokescreen for creditors, Donna could place title to her home in a land trust and then execute a mortgage for $250,000 in favor of one of her LLCs. See Figure 8.2.

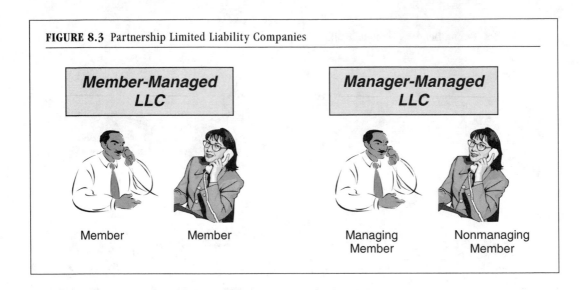

FIGURE 8.3 Partnership Limited Liability Companies

The Partnership

Let's look at another common business arrangement—the partnership. Most people in business together operate as a general partnership. As discussed earlier, the general partnership can be disastrous if your partner commits a wrongdoing for which you are held liable.

The limited liability company can be a very useful tool for partners, depending on the nature of the business. The LLC offers liability protection, ease of operation, and flexibility in management. Following are two such examples, using an LLC. See Figure 8.3.

In the member-managed example, both owners (members) have the authority to deal with the public and act on behalf of the company. In the manager-managed example, only the managing member has the authority to act on behalf of the company; the nonmanaging member is a silent partner, similar to a limited partner.

If a substantial portion of the company's business is personal services, then all of the income of the members could be subject to self-employment tax. In such a case, a corporation might be a better vehicle. Once again, there is no one-size-fits-all, so review the appropriate issues with your tax advisor.

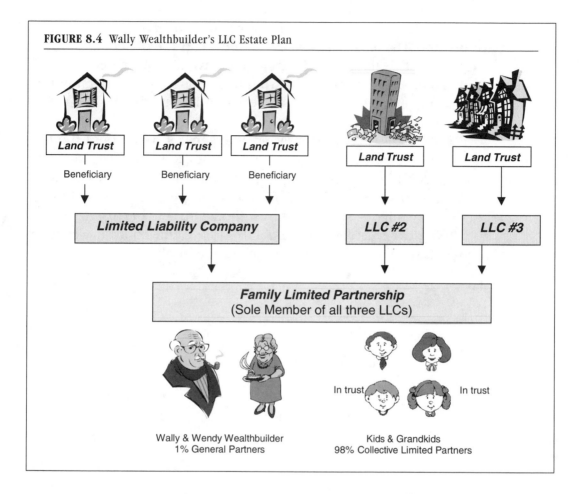

FIGURE 8.4 Wally Wealthbuilder's LLC Estate Plan

The Estate Planner

Our final example is Wally Wealthbuilder, a wealthy grandparent with a vast real estate empire. He has multiple properties, including an apartment building, single-family homes, and several duplexes. He is married with a daughter who is also married. He has two minor grandchildren. His concerns are asset protection, estate taxes, and control of assets while he is still alive. See Figure 8.4.

In this scenario, the properties are titled separately in land trusts for privacy. The beneficiaries of the land trusts are divided into three LLCs to limit Wally's risk of exposure to lawsuits. All three LLCs are single member; that is, they share the common owner, a family limited partnership. For federal income tax and estate planning, the FLP is the "owner" of all the properties.

Wally and his wife, Wendy, are the general partners of the FLP and have full control of the assets while they are alive. The children and grandchildren are limited partners, so the bulk of the estate does not belong to Wally and Wendy for estate tax purposes. Note that the children are minors, so their interest should be held in trust, their parents being the trustees. (If the children have full control over their partnership interest, they may do something foolish!)

CHAPTER 9

Estate Planning Strategies

This chapter will explain some nifty estate planning strategies available with limited partnerships and limited liability companies.

Essentially, *estate planning* is the process of planning for the transfer of your assets to your heirs. Estate planning includes three basic issues:

1. Minimizing estate taxes

2. Keeping your assets, particularly your business, from being impaired while your affairs are being resolved

3. Avoiding the expense and hassle of probate

Keep in mind that estate planning, tax planning, and asset protection often go hand in hand. In most cases, the three areas will complement each other. In some cases, there will be a trade-off between tax advantages, estate planning, and asset protection. Therefore, it is recommended that you contact your attorney and/or tax advisor before proceeding.

Basic Estate Planning Issues

The Unified Credit

As of tax year 2003, you may leave up to $1,000,000 worth of assets to your heirs without any federal estate tax. The $1,000,000 credit will increase until 2010, at which time the federal estate tax exemption is unlimited. (This unlimited exemption lasts just one year and is up for discussion and complete revision by Congress.) Every dollar of assets left in your taxable estate beyond the unified credit is eaten at graduated tax rates as high as 55 percent.

The Unlimited Marital Deduction

You may pass any amount of assets to your spouse without paying estate taxes. This does not affect the unified credit exemption, which can be used in conjunction with the marital deduction.

Gifts and the Unified Credit

Even in America, you cannot transfer all of your assets to your heirs while you are alive without taxable consequences. You can make a gift of up to $11,000 per year to an unlimited number of people (related or unrelated to you) without paying gift tax. If you give a gift of more than $11,000 in one year to any one person, your unified credit is reduced. The reason for the name *unified* credit is that it is a combination of both lifetime and testamentary transfers. You are obligated to file a gift tax return with the IRS each time you gift more than $11,000 in one tax year to a single person, so they can keep tabs on your unified credit. Thus, beyond the $11,000 per year exclusion, you can give gifts totaling $1,000,000 over your life without paying tax (year 2003 rates). However, when you die, your exemption will be used up. In that case, *everything* left in your estate is subject to estate tax, except what is left to your spouse.

If you are making gifts to your children, your spouse can join you so that you can give up to $22,000 per year per child without paying gift tax. The good news is, all gifts between spouses are exempt from gift tax.

Minimizing Estate Taxes with Gifts of Partnership and LLC Interests

For estate tax purposes, you are not taxed on items that are not in your estate. You can certainly use the annual gift exemptions to help accomplish this goal. However, making gifts presents two major challenges:

1. Large assets, such as a family business and real estate, are difficult to transfer in small parts.

2. You lose control of the asset once it is gifted.

The limited partnership and LLC help solve both of these challenges in that they permit you to divide an asset into pieces. For example, a parcel of real estate can be transferred in parts, but this would require a new deed each year to transfer a small percentage of the property. If the property were transferred into an LLC, the yearly gift can be accomplished by a transfer of an interest in the LLC, not the real estate itself.

Second, you can retain control of the asset by remaining a general partner, or in the case of an LLC, the manager. If properly structured, you can give as much as 99 percent of your limited partnership or LLC interests to your heirs, yet still remain in full control of the assets of the partnership or LLC.

Here is an example:

Fred and Connie's estate consists of a successful family business worth $2,500,000. On Fred and Connie's untimely demise, their estate would be subject to a substantial tax. Fred and Connie fear that there would not be enough cash in the estate to pay the estate tax on $1,500,000. Fred and Connie do not want their business, for which they worked years to create, to be forced into liquidation to pay the IRS.

Fred and Connie go to an estate planning seminar and learn that they can make gifts of their assets to reduce their estate and thus their estate tax liability. They want to leave the business to their children but do not want them to have the ability to liquidate the business while Fred and Connie are still alive.

Fred and Connie can accomplish their goals with a limited partnership. They would each be 1 percent general partners and 49 percent limited partners. Each year, Connie and Fred could gift limited partnership shares worth $22,000 to each child, tax-free. As limited partners, the children will have limited rights to demand liquidation of the partnership. Fred and Connie, as general partners, will have full control of the partnership until they both die. Their estate will be substantially reduced by the annual gifts of partnership interests to their children. (They could accomplish the same goals with an LLC, wherein they retain control as managers of the company.)

Making Young Children Partners in Your Business

If you make your minor children partners in your business, you will need to establish a custodianship or trust to hold the interest for the benefit of the children. This technique should not be attempted without the assistance of a qualified attorney.

Valuation Discounts

Lack of Marketability

Limited partners generally have no right to demand distributions of income, participate in management, or force a liquidation of the partnership. Similarly, members of an LLC who are not managers cannot demand distributions of income, participate in management, or force a liquidation of the company. This lack of power results in a lack of value for the partnership or membership interest. That is, if a limited partner or member tried to sell his or her interest, no one in his or her right mind would pay full value for the interest, especially in the case of a family partnership. This lack of marketability for the partnership or LLC share is taken into consideration for estate tax purposes. In the example above, the owners of a family business gifted limited partnership shares to their children on an annual basis. When either parent dies, his or her remaining limited partnership share is subject to a substantial discount (as much as 20 to 30 percent) for lack of marketability.

Minority Interest Discount

Furthermore, if the deceased parent's remaining interest is a minority share, there is an additional discount, because the interest lacks the controlling vote. The discount for a minority interest may be another 20 to 30 percent. Keep in mind, however, that while the minority-holding member is alive, he or she may still have *effective* control by acting as the general partner or manager.

Leveraging Your Gifts

Because gifts up to $11,000 per year to any person are exempt from taxation, you can combine this strategy with the LLC or limited partnership for maximum effectiveness. A membership or partnership interest already has a reduced valuation (see discussion above), so an effective gift of as much as $22,000 per year can be made. In other words, a gift of partnership or membership interest that has a "book value" of $22,000 may be made with a discounted tax value of closer to $11,000. I recommend that you retain professional counsel before attempting to use this powerful technique.

Warning on Family Partnerships

The IRS closely scrutinizes family partnerships, particularly the annual gift exclusion. You must be able to show that there was a completed gift. Retention of income, undue control over partnership assets, and forbidding your children from selling their shares may result in an incomplete gift. See your legal advisor before attempting any of these strategies.

Avoiding Ancillary Probate

Probate is that long, expensive, and painful process of proving a will and settling the deceased's financial affairs. If the deceased owns property in other states, a proceeding, called "ancillary probate," must be completed in each state.

Once you transfer your assets to a limited partnership or LLC, your interest is considered "intangible personal property." This type of property goes where you go. Thus, if all of your assets are held in partnerships or LLCs, your assets will become localized to where you reside. Ancillary probate is avoided.

Continuity of Business

A death in a family business can often lead to financial disaster. Without proper planning, a business can be wiped out because the estate is not liquid enough to pay its taxes. Without a will, a personal representative must be appointed by the court to oversee the business while the decedent's estate is resolved. The assets, which used to belong to the decedent, are in control of a court-appointed representative, not the heirs. The probate process could take months, even years to complete. In the meantime, the business falls apart.

Establishing a business as an entity apart from its owner will prevent this kind of disruption. Generally, the death of a general partner of a limited partnership or member of an LLC will dissolve the business. However, most properly drafted agreements permit the surviving partners or members to continue the business. In addition, the assets of the business belong to the partnership or LLC, not the deceased. The deceased's interest in the partnership or LLC is part of his estate. The personal representative appointed by the court is not in control of the business.

CHAPTER 10

More Legal Issues

Even if you do everything right, you can still get sued. It is also possible that a creditor's attorney could get through your armor and get to you personally. No matter how much you plan, a judge may simply rule against you because he or she doesn't like you. The judge may ignore the law and hold you personally liable for a debt. It isn't fair, but it sometimes can happen. When Plan A doesn't work, you need a Plan B.

Bankruptcy

Federal bankruptcy protection can sometimes be your only choice. The bankruptcy laws are often twisted and abused by people, but they are a legitimate means of dealing with an overwhelming amount of debt or liability. Bankruptcy can also be an effective negotiating device for a creditor that fears losing his or her money.

The three basic types of bankruptcy processes are Chapter 7, Chapter 11, and Chapter 13.

Chapter 7 Bankruptcy

Chapter 7 bankruptcy is also known as "straight liquidation," which means all of your debts are wiped out. In addition, all of your nonexempt assets are sold to pay your creditors. The exemptions are somewhat state specific, depending on where you live.

The filing of a petition under Chapter 7 "automatically stays" most actions against the debtor or the debtor's property. The "stay" is a legal halt to all creditors' efforts. As long as the stay is in effect, creditors cannot start or continue any lawsuits or collections or even make demands for payments. All of the creditors usually receive notice of the filing of the petition from the clerk of the federal bankruptcy court. If they don't, you can always fax a copy of the petition to the creditor seeking collection.

The commencement of a bankruptcy case creates an "estate." The estate technically becomes the temporary legal owner of all of the debtor's property. An impartial case trustee is appointed by the U.S. trustee to administer the case and liquidate assets to pay creditors.

A "meeting of creditors" is usually held about 45 days after the bankruptcy petition is filed. At the meeting, the creditors may appear and ask questions regarding the debtor's financial affairs and property. In most consumer cases, the debt consists mainly of credit card obligations, so the creditors won't show up. The trustee may also question the debtor about his or her obligations.

Within a few months (sooner or later, depending on your area), the court will approve or deny the discharge of debt. A Chapter 7 discharge is a "clean slate," which can only be done once every seven years.

Certain debts are not dischargeable in Chapter 7 bankruptcy, including federal income taxes assessed in the last three years, child support payments, government fines, debt procured as a result of fraud, and payroll taxes.

A free copy of the official U.S. Bankruptcy Court forms can be downloaded from the Internet at <www.uscourts.gov/bankform>.

Chapters 11 and 13 Bankruptcy

Chapter 13 bankruptcy is known as a "wage earner's plan," a "reorganization" in legal terms. The filing of a petition under Chapter 13 also automatically stays actions against the debtor or the debtor's property. Unlike a Chapter 7 plan, the debtor remains in possession of his or her assets. The debtor comes up with a plan to continue paying debts as well as any arrears over a three- to five-year period. It is essentially a payment plan forced on the creditors. Many debts that are not dischargeable under Chapter 7 may be reorganized under Chapter 13.

Corporate debtors and individuals with unsecured debts greater than $250,000 or secured debts greater than $750,000 must file for bankruptcy under Chapter 11. If a plan is not approved by the court under Chapters 11 or 13, the debtor can convert to a Chapter 7.

As of the date of this publication, the U.S. Congress was considering a major overhaul of the bankruptcy laws to make it more difficult to file for discharge. You can read more on the Internet at <www .abiworld.org>.

The IRS as a Creditor

The IRS is essentially the same as any other creditor, except it does not have to go to court to obtain a judgment. The IRS files a "Notice of Federal Tax Lien" in the counties it believes you own property. Before the IRS files a lien, it must assess the liability and send you a notice and demand for payment. If you don't respond, the lien gets filed.

Generally, there is a three-year statute of limitations for the IRS auditing your tax return. The statute of limitations is six years if you fail to report income in excess of 25 percent of the amount stated on your return. There is no statute of limitations in the case of a false or fraudulent tax return filed with the IRS with intent to evade any tax.

The IRS has an "Offer in Compromise" program that allows you to settle your unpaid debt for less than it claims you owe. However, if you willfully neglected to file your tax returns for a number of years, you cannot make an offer in compromise. In addition, the IRS can criminally prosecute you. If you owe a substantial amount of money and/or are facing possible criminal charges, you should hire a competent tax attorney to represent you in dealing with the IRS.

Insurance

When I present seminars on the topic of asset protection, a common question I hear is: "Now that I am incorporated, should I cancel my insurance?" To the other extreme, a common remark made by ignorant tax professionals and attorneys is: "Don't bother with corporations, just buy a lot of insurance." Both of these approaches are dangerous.

Insurance should never be overlooked as a means of protection. Insurance will cover many claims of a *tortious* nature (slip-and-fall, negligence, etc). The fact that you have insurance to cover these types of claims will help if your corporation is undercapitalized. If you do not have insurance and someone who is injured sues your "shell" corporation, a court may think you were not "playing fair." This is particularly important if your business is engaged in activities that are dangerous or hazardous to the public.

Insurance will not typically cover breach of contract claims, but courts are less likely to set aside a corporation for these types of debts. However, claims such as sexual harassment, employment discrimination, wrongful termination, and fraud are almost never covered by insurance.

Another benefit of insurance is that the duty of an insurance company to "defend" (pay for your legal defense) is much broader than its duty to "indemnify" (pay for a judgment against you). Legal fees alone can be painful, especially for frivolous lawsuits, even if you win in court. The court rarely awards the defending party legal fees, and the plaintiff's lawyer is often working on a contingent-fee basis, so the plaintiff himself has nothing to lose by suing your company. (Have you ever heard the expression, "Never get into a fight with an ugly person because he has nothing to lose"?)

Review your policies with your insurance agent as to coverage issues and policy limits. If cost is an issue, increase your deductible. A lower deductible on a policy is generally more expensive than a higher coverage limit for liability. Following is a brief summary of available insurance for your protection.

General Business Liability Insurance

This type of insurance can be reasonable and will cover a wide range of lawsuits from personal injury claims to copyright violations. Obviously, the higher the deductible, the cheaper the insurance. It may be worthwhile to keep an insurance policy with a large deductible and high limits to substitute for having to keep excess capital in your corporation.

Malpractice Insurance

Lawyers, doctors, engineers, architects, real estate brokers, and other professionals can obtain malpractice or "errors and omissions" insurance. This insurance covers goof-ups that you and your employees may make in dealing with clients. This insurance can be very expensive, depending on the kind of business you are involved in. In addition, the coverage is weak, because the policies are often "claims made"; that is, they only cover claims made in the year the policy is in effect. Regular liability insurance will cover you if you are sued years later for events that occurred during the policy period. In many states, the statute of limitations for malpractice is six years, so a lawsuit years later will not be covered if you do not maintain continuous coverage.

Director Liability Insurance

Director liability can be so precarious that many people refuse to serve on the board of any corporation without director liability insurance. This insurance is expensive and may not be necessary for a small corporation.

Umbrella Liability Insurance

An umbrella policy is one that kicks in after all other underlying coverage is exhausted. For example, if you have a general liability policy with $100,000 and a judgment is rendered against your corporation for $500,000, the umbrella policy kicks in the extra $400,000. Umbrella insurance does not cover other claims that are otherwise not insured (e.g., breach of contract claim). Most insurance companies require that you maintain all of your insurance with their company before they will issue an umbrella policy. Umbrella policies are quite reasonable and can cover your business for up to several million dollars.

Extended Homeowners Insurance

A typical homeowners policy will cover basic liability claims against you regarding the property. It will not cover general liability claims unrelated to your property. For example, if you injure another while riding your Jet Ski on a nearby lake, this claim will not be covered unless your homeowners policy has a special endorsement.

Fraudulent Conveyances

As we discussed in the Introduction, fraudulent conveyance laws will scrutinize transfers made while a lawsuit is looming. Virtually anything you do while facing a lawsuit or liability will be deemed suspect. In addition, fraudulent conveyance laws may be used by a creditor to set aside a transfer you made without any fraudulent intent and before you even knew you would be sued.

Generally, any conveyances made for less than fair market value may be considered fraudulent (and thus voidable at the request of a creditor), if such a transfer makes you broke and leaves you with insufficient capital to meet your future debts or soon thereafter results in unreasonably large liabilities. Gifts between family members are virtually always considered suspect.

The statute of limitations for fraudulent conveyances (i.e., the time period for which conveyances are deemed suspect and voidable) generally runs from two to six years, depending on state law. In some instances, a fraudulent conveyance can subject you to criminal liability, especially if you try to defraud a creditor in bankruptcy.

So how do you get around these rules? Implement these strategies now, and do it for a reason other than simply to protect yourself from creditors. Everyone has the right to limit liability. After all, isn't that the purpose of a corporation? However, to avoid the pitfalls of fraudulent conveyances, you should combine an asset protection plan with the following:

- A valid business purposes (e.g., the "prestige" of a corporation)

- An estate plan

- Gift or charitable purpose

- Income tax reduction

If a creditor claims that you transferred assets fraudulently, you will have other valid reasons to justify the transfer. For example, if you placed most of your assets into an irrevocable trust for the benefit of your children, your intent was "estate planning." If you transferred all of the assets of your unincorporated business into a corporation and continued the same business under the corporate entity, your intent was "tax savings." You get the picture?

Do not transfer everything at once. As stated above, a transfer may be considered fraudulent if it makes you broke. If you transfer everything at once, you are broke. Transfer assets in chunks, so that the earliest transfers will be harder to challenge.

Another important consideration is to spread wealth out both geographically and among several people or entities. The more your wealth is broken up and spread apart, the more difficult it is for a creditor to attack and prove the transfers were fraudulent. The very fact that a creditor has to go to another state to get your assets will greatly impede his or her efforts. A judgment from one state is enforceable in another state, but there are still procedural hoops a creditor must jump through. Every hoop costs the creditor more money and buys you more time.

I cannot stress enough that you stick to your plan. An asset protection plan does not have to be complicated; it just has to be followed. Remember your ABCs of wealth protection and you will sleep safe, knowing that you and your assets are "untouchable." Do it right and do it NOW!

What to Do Next

Now that you are armed with this valuable information, where do you go from here?

Visit with an Attorney

Consider visiting a local attorney who is well versed in asset protection strategies. This may not be easy, because few attorneys specialize in this field of endeavor. Check the state bar directory under "estate planning" and "bankruptcy" for referrals. If the attorney you meet with knows less than you have learned from this book, find another attorney!

Books and Seminars

Many books and seminars are published on the topic of asset protection, but it takes some knowledge to determine which are reputable and knowledgeable. Many of these seminars are intended solely to entice you into purchasing an offshore trust, Nevada corporation, or other service. I am not necessarily saying none of these angles are legitimate, but be leery of anyone who promotes a one-size-fits-all approach.

The bottom line: Read a lot, educate yourself, ask lot of questions, and do what is best for *you*!

A PPENDIX

105

State Homestead Law Exemptions

The following is a brief summary of homestead exemptions by state with references to state statutes. In some states, husband and wife may claim a separate exemption and the exemption may be limited to acreage of a certain size. It is important that you review the law in your state with an attorney who is familiar with homestead law (and Federal Bankruptcy Law) and the particular requirements for utilizing the exemption in your state. A state-by-state summary of exemptions is available at <www.bankruptcyaction.com/exemptionsnonjava.htm>.

STATE	EXEMPTION	STATE STATUTE
Alabama	$5,000 (double for husband & wife)	A.C. §6-10-2
Alaska	$54,000	A.S. §9.38.010
Arizona	$100,000 (acreage restriction)	A.R.S. §33-1121.01
Arkansas	Unlimited value (acreage restriction)	Ark. Const. §9-3, 4, 5
California	$17,425–$100,000, depending on age, marital status & income	Cal Code Civ Pro §704.710 through 704.730
Colorado	$30,000	C.R.S. §38-41-201
Connecticut	$75,000	C.G.S.A. §52-352b(t)
Delaware	None	
D.C.	None	
Florida	Unlimited value (acreage restriction)	F.S.A. §222.01 through .05
Georgia	$5,000	G.C.A. §44-13-100(a)(1)
Hawaii	$20,000–$30,000 depending on age (acreage restriction)	H.R.S. §36-651-91, 92, 96
Idaho	$50,000	I.C. §55-1003, 1113
Illinois	$7,500	I.A.S. §735-5/12-901, 906
Indiana	$7,500	I.S.A. §34-2-28-1(a)(1)
Iowa	Unlimited value (acreage restriction)	I.C.A. §499A.18, 561.2
Kansas	Unlimited value (acreage restriction)	K.S.A. §60-2301
Kentucky	$5,000	K.R.S. §427.060, 427.090

STATE	EXEMPTION	STATE STATUTE
Louisiana	$15,000 (acreage restriction)	L.R.S.A. §20-1
Maine	$12,500–$60,000 depending on age; Joint owner/debtors can double	M.R.S.A. §14-4422(1)
Maryland	None	
Massachusetts	$100,000–$200,000 depending on age	M.G.L.A. §188-1, 1A
Michigan	$3,500 (acreage restriction)	M.C.L. §559.214,600.6023
Minnesota	$200,000 (acreage restriction)	M.S.A. §510.01, .02
Mississippi	$75,000 (acreage and age restriction)	M.C. §85-3-1(b)(I)
Missouri	$8,000	Ann M.S. §513.430(6)
Montana	$40,000	M.C.A. §70-32-104, 201
Nebraska	$10,000 (acreage restriction)	R.S.N. §40-101, 111, 113
Nevada	$125,000	N.R.S.A. §21.090(1)(m), 115.010
New Hampshire	$30,000	N.H.R.S.A. §480:1
New Jersey	None	
New Mexico	$30,000 (joint owner/debtors may double)	N.M.S.A. §42-10-9
New York	$10,000 (married couples may double)	N.Y.C.P.L.R. §5206
N. Carolina	$10,000	G.S.N.C. §1c-1601(a)(1)(2)
N. Dakota	$80,000	N.D.C.C. §28-22-02(10)
Ohio	$5,000	O.R.C. §2329.66(A)(1)(b)
Oklahoma	Unlimited (acreage restriction)	O.S.A. §31-1(A)(1)
Oregon	$25,000 ($33,000 for joint debtor/owners; acreage restriction)	O.R.S. §23.164, 23.445
Penn.	None	
Rhode Island	None	
S. Carolina	$5,000 (double for joint debtor/owners)	Code of Laws S.C. §15-41-30(1)
S. Dakota	Unlimited (acreage restriction)	S.D.C.L. §43-3-1, 2, 3, 4

STATE	EXEMPTION	STATE STATUTE
Tennessee	$5,000 ($7,500 for joint debtor/ owners)	T.C.A. §26-2-301
Texas	Unlimited (acreage restriction)	T.R.C.S.A. §41.001, .002
Utah	$8,000 + $2,000 for spouse + $500 per dependent	U.C. §78-23-2
Vermont	$30,000	V.S.A. §27-101
Virginia	$5,000 + $500 per dependent	Code of Va. §34-4, 18, 20
Washington	$30,000	R.C.W.A. §6.13.010, .030
W. Virginia	$15,000	W.V.C. §38-10-4(a)
Wisconsin	$40,000	W.S.A. §815.20
Wyoming	$10,000 (double for joint debtor/ owners)	W.S.A. §1-20-101, 102

Federal Bankruptcy Exemptions
11 United States Code §522

HOMESTEAD:

- Real property, including co-op or mobile home, to $15,000; unused portion of homestead to $75,000 may be applied to any property.

INSURANCE:

- Disability, illness, or unemployment benefits
- Life insurance payments for person you depended on, needed for support
- Life insurance policy with loan value, in accrued dividends or interest, to $8,000
- Unmatured life insurance contract, except credit insurance policy

MISCELLANEOUS:

- Alimony, child support needed for support

PENSIONS:

- ERISA-qualified benefits needed for support

PERSONAL PROPERTY:

- Animals, crops, clothing, appliances, books, furnishings, household goods, musical instruments to 400 per item, $8,000 total
- Health aids
- Jewelry to $1,000
- Lost earnings payments
- Motor vehicle to $2,400
- Personal injury recoveries to $15,000 (not to include pain and suffering or pecuniary loss)
- Wrongful death recoveries for person you depended on

PUBLIC BENEFITS:

- Crime victims' compensation
- Public assistance
- Social Security
- Unemployment compensation
- Veterans' benefits

TOOLS OF TRADE:

- Implements, books, and tools of trade to $1,500

Excerpts from Sample Fraudulent Transfer Law
(Colorado Uniform Fraudulent Transfer Act Title 38, Chapter 8)

38-8-105. Transfers fraudulent as to present and future creditors.

(1) A transfer made or obligation incurred by a debtor is fraudulent as to a creditor, whether the creditor's claim arose before or after the transfer was made or the obligation was incurred, if the debtor made the transfer or incurred the obligation:

(a) With actual intent to hinder, delay, or defraud any creditor of the debtor; or

(b) Without receiving a reasonably equivalent value in exchange for the transfer or obligation, and the debtor:

(I) Was engaged or was about to engage in a business or a transaction for which the remaining assets of the debtor were unreasonably small in relation to the business or transaction; or

(II) Intended to incur, or believed or reasonably should have believed that he would incur, debts beyond his ability to pay as they became due.

(2) In determining actual intent under paragraph (a) of subsection (1) of this section, consideration may be given, among other factors, to whether:

(a) The transfer or obligation was to an insider;

(b) The debtor retained possession or control of the property transferred after the transfer;

(c) The transfer or obligation was disclosed or concealed;

(d) Before the transfer was made or obligation was incurred, the debtor had been sued or threatened with suit;

(e) The transfer was of substantially all the debtor's assets;

(f) The debtor absconded;

(g) The debtor removed or concealed assets;

(h) The value of the consideration received by the debtor was reasonably equivalent to the value of the asset transferred or the amount of the obligation incurred;

(i) The debtor was insolvent or became insolvent shortly after the transfer was made or the obligation was incurred;

(j) The transfer occurred shortly before or shortly after a substantial debt was incurred; and

(k) The debtor transferred the essential assets of the business to a lienor who transferred the assets to an insider of the debtor.

38-8-106. Transfers fraudulent as to present creditors.

(1) A transfer made or obligation incurred by a debtor is fraudulent as to a creditor whose claim arose before the transfer was made or the obligation was incurred if the debtor made the transfer or incurred the obligation without receiving a reasonably equivalent value in exchange for the transfer or obligation and the debtor was insolvent at that time or the debtor became insolvent as a result of the transfer or obligation.

(2) A transfer made by a debtor is fraudulent as to a creditor whose claim arose before the transfer was made if the transfer was made to an insider for an antecedent debt, the debtor was insolvent at that time, and the insider had reasonable cause to believe that the debtor was insolvent.

38-8-107. When transfer is made or obligation is incurred.

(1) For the purposes of this article:

(a) A transfer is made:

(I) With respect to an asset that is real property other than a fixture, but including the interest of a seller or purchaser under a contract for the sale of the asset, when the transfer is so far perfected that a good-faith purchaser of the asset from the debtor against whom applicable law permits the transfer to be perfected cannot acquire an interest in the asset that is superior to the interest of the transferee; and

(II) With respect to an asset that is not real property or that is a fixture, when the transfer is so far perfected that a creditor on a simple contract cannot acquire a judicial lien otherwise than under this article that is superior to the interest of the transferee.

(2) If applicable law permits the transfer to be perfected as provided in subsection (1) of this section and the transfer is not so perfected before the commencement of an action for relief under this article, the transfer is deemed made immediately before the commencement of the action.

(3) If applicable law does not permit the transfer to be perfected as provided in subsection (1) of this section, the transfer is made when it becomes effective between the debtor and the transferee.

(4) A transfer is not made until the debtor has acquired rights in the asset transferred.

(5) An obligation is incurred:
  (a) If oral, when it becomes effective between the parties; or
  (b) If evidenced by a writing, when the writing executed by the obligor is delivered to or for the benefit of the obligee.

38-8-108. Remedies of creditors.

(1) In an action for relief against a transfer or obligation under this article, a creditor, subject to the limitations in section 38-8-109, may obtain:
  (a) Avoidance of the transfer or obligation to the extent necessary to satisfy the creditor's claim;
  (b) An attachment or other provisional remedy against the asset transferred or other property of the transferee in accordance with the procedure prescribed by the Colorado rules of civil procedure;
  (c) Subject to applicable principles of equity and in accordance with applicable rules of civil procedure:
    (I) An injunction against further disposition by the debtor or a transferee, or both, of the asset transferred or of other property;
    (II) Appointment of a receiver to take charge of the asset transferred or of other property of the transferee; or
    (III) Any other relief the circumstances may require.

(2) If a creditor has obtained a judgment on a claim against the debtor, the creditor, if the court so orders, may levy execution on the asset transferred or its proceeds.

Excerpts from California Community Property Law

A. Except as otherwise expressly provided by statute, the community property is liable for a debt incurred by either spouse before or after marriage, regardless which spouse has the management and control of the property and regardless whether one or both spouses are parties to the debt or to a judgment for the debt.

B. The earnings of a married person during marriage are not liable for a debt incurred by the person's spouse before marriage . . . they remain not liable so long as they are held in a deposit account in which the person's spouse has no right of withdrawal and are uncommingled with other community property, except property insignificant in amount.

•   •   •

A. A married person is not liable for any injury or damage caused by the other spouse except in cases where he or she would be liable therefor if the marriage did not exist.

B. The liability of a married person for death or injury to person or property shall be satisfied as follows:

1. If the liability of the married person is based upon an act or omission which occurred while the married person was performing an activity for the benefit of the community, the liability shall first be satisfied from the community property and second from the separate property of the married person.

2. If the liability of the married person is not based upon an act or omission which occurred while the married person was performing an activity for the benefit of the community, the liability shall first be satisfied from the separate property of the married person and second from the community property.

Abusive Trust Tax Evasion Schemes—Special Types of Trusts (from www.IRS.gov)

Special Types of Trusts

Common Law Trust

Contrary to the claims of promoters, "common law trusts" no longer exist since all states now have statutes relating to the creation and operation of trusts.

Foreign Trust

Through 1996, a trust was foreign if the trustee, corpus, and administration were foreign. Since 1996, a trust is foreign unless a U.S. court supervises the trust and a U.S. fiduciary controls all substantial decisions. U.S. taxpayers are subject to filing Form 3520, *Creation of or Transfer to Certain Foreign Trusts,* Form 3520-A, *Annual Return of Foreign Trust with U.S. Beneficiaries,* and Form 926, *Return by a Transferor of Property to a Foreign Estate or Trust,* when contributing property to a foreign trust. These trusts are usually U.S. tax neutral and are treated as grantor trusts with income taxed to the grantor.

Foreign trusts that have income attributable to U.S. sources and are not grantor trusts are required to file Form 1040NR, U.S. Nonresident Alien Income Tax Return. Foreign trusts that have income attributable to U.S. sources and are grantor trusts would have that income directly attributable to the grantor (if U.S. grantor income, it must be included on Form 1040; if nonresident alien grantor income, it must be included on Form 1040NR).

Personal Residence Trust

A personal residence trust involves the transfer of a personal residence to a trust with the grantor retaining the right to live in the residence for a fixed term of years. Upon the shorter of the grantor's death or the expiration of the term of years, title to the residence passes to beneficiaries of the trust. This is an irrevocable trust with gift tax implications.

Qualified Personal Residence Trust
A qualified personal residence trust involves the transfer of a personal residence to a trust with the grantor retaining a qualified term interest . . . If the grantor dies before the end of the qualified term interest, the value of the residence is included in the grantor's estate. If the grantor survives to the end of the qualified term interest, the residence passes to beneficiaries of the trust. A QPRT is a grantor trust, with special valuation rules for estate and gift tax purposes, governed under IRC 2702.

Grantor Retained Income Trust
In a grantor retained income trust, the grantor creates an irrevocable trust and retains the right to all trust income for: (a) the earlier of a specified term or the death of the grantor; or (b) a specified term. If the grantor survives the specified term, the trust principal passes to others according to the terms and provisions of the trust instrument. For federal tax purposes, this trust is treated as a grantor trust.

Grantor Retained Annuity Trust
In a grantor retained annuity trust, the grantor creates an irrevocable trust and retains the right to receive, for a specified term, an annuity based on specified sum or fixed percentage of the value of the assets transferred to the trust. A grantor retained annuity trust is specifically authorized by Internal Revenue Code Section 2702(a)(2)(B) and 2702(b). For federal tax purposes, this trust is treated as a grantor trust.

Grantor Retained Unitrust
A grantor retained unitrust is similar to a grantor retained annuity trust. However, in a grantor retained unitrust, the grantor creates an irrevocable trust and retains, for a specified term, an annual right to receive a fixed percentage of the annually determined net fair market value of the trust assets (Treasury Regulation Section 25.2702-(c)(1)). For federal tax purposes, this trust is treated as a grantor trust.

Charitable Trusts

- **Charitable Lead Trust**
  A charitable lead trust pays an annuity or unitrust interest to a designated charity for a specified term of years (the "charitable term") with the remainder ultimately distributed to noncharitable beneficiaries. There is no specified limit for the charitable term. The donor receives a charitable deduction for the value of the interest received by the charity. The value of the noncharitable beneficiary's remainder interest is a taxable gift by the grantor.

- **Charitable Lead Annuity Trust**
  A charitable lead annuity trust is a charitable lead trust paying a fixed percentage of the initial value of the trust assets to the charity for the charitable term.

- **Charitable Lead Unitrust**
  A charitable lead unitrust is a charitable lead trust paying a percentage of the value of its assets, determined annually, to a charity for the charitable term.

- **Charitable Remainder Trust**
  In a charitable remainder trust, the donor transfers assets to an annuity trust or unitrust. The trust pays the donor or another beneficiary a certain amount each year for a specified period. In an annuity trust, the payment is a specified dollar amount. In a unitrust, the payment is a percentage of the value of the trust, as valued each year. The term of the trust is limited to 20 years or the life of the designated recipients. At the end of the term of the trust, the remaining trust assets must be distributed to a charitable organization. Contributions to the charitable remainder trust can qualify for a charitable deduction (limited to the present value of the charitable organization's remainder interest). Revenue Procedures 89-20, 89-21, 90-30,

and 90-31 provide sample trust forms that the Service will recognize as meeting charitable remainder trust requirements.

- **Pooled Income Fund Trust**
  A pooled income fund is an unincorporated fund set up by a public charity to which a person transfers property, reserving an income interest in, and giving the charity the remainder interest in that property. The Code and Regulations under Section 642 establish trust requirements. These funds file Form 1041.

Life Insurance Trust

An insurance trust is generally an irrevocable trust that owns insurance on the life of the grantor or grantor and spouse. The trust is designed to avoid federal estate taxation of the insurance proceeds on the deaths of the grantor or spouse. When premium payments or other gifts to the trust are made, the trust instrument grants specified beneficiaries Crummey withdrawal rights over the gifts so that they will qualify for the federal gift tax annual exclusion. These trusts would generally file a Form 1041 as a complex trust, if the $600 income requirement were met.

Qualified Subchapter S Trust (QSST)

A QSST is a statutory creature established by IRC Section 1361(d)(3). By meeting the requirements of a QSST, a trust may own S Corporation shares. An election must be made to be treated as a QSST and once made is irrevocable.

Electing Small Business Trust (ESBT)

An ESBT is a statutory creature established by IRC Section 641(d). By meeting the requirements of an ESBT, a trust may own S Corporation shares. ESBTs must file Form 1041 and the S Corporation income is taxed at the trust's highest marginal rate. No income distribution deduction is allowed to beneficiaries. To be treated as an ESBT, an election must be made.

Funeral Trust

This is an arrangement between the grantor and funeral home/cemetery to allow for the prepayment of funeral expenses. The funeral trust is a "pooled income fund" set up by a funeral home/cemetery to which a person transfers property to cover future funeral and burial costs. These are grantor trusts with the grantor responsible for reporting income. The trustee may make an election on qualified preneed funeral trusts to not be treated as a grantor trust, with the tax being paid by the trustee.

Rabbi Trust

An irrevocable trust that functions as a type of retirement plan or deferred compensation arrangement that offers a limited amount of security to the deferring employee.

Business Trust

The term "business trust" is not used in the Internal Revenue Code. The regulations require that trusts operating a trade or business be treated as a corporation, partnership, or sole proprietorship, if the grantor, beneficiary, or fiduciary materially participates in the operations or daily management of the business. If the grantor maintains control of the trust, then grantor trust rules will apply. Otherwise, the trust would be treated as a simple or complex trust, depending on the trust instrument.

Pure Trust

The term "pure trust" is not used in the Internal Revenue Code. Whatever the name of the arrangement, however, the taxation of the entity must comply with the requirements of the Internal Revenue Code. The requirements are based on the economic reality of the arrangement, not its nomenclature. If the pure trust meets the definition of a trust, then it would be taxed under simple, complex, or grantor trust rules, depending on the trust instrument.

Illinois Land Trust

In Illinois, and in five other states, legislation has been enacted that creates a special type of trust, commonly referred to as an "Illinois Land Trust." These trusts are designed to house real estate within a grantor trust and provide limited access to grantor or beneficiary information contained in the trust instrument or known to the trustee. Once a land trust is established, the ability to trace property transactions becomes limited as state law establishes the right of the trustee not to disclose the true owner of the property or those with a beneficial interest. The "land trust" has no special distinction in the Internal Revenue Code and would be a simple, complex, or grantor trust depending on the terms of the trust instrument. Filing requirements would depend on the type of trust.

Delaware Business Trust or Alaska Business Trust

A trust established to hold and invest assets with greater flexibility than allowed by most trusts. Permits limited liability, creditor protection, and valuation discounts. These trusts are a creation of the Delaware and Alaska legislatures and have no impact on taxation of trusts for federal purposes. These "business trusts" have no special distinction in the Internal Revenue Code and would be a simple, complex, or grantor trust depending on the terms of the trust instrument. The regulations require that trusts operating a trade or business be treated as a corporation, partnership, or sole proprietorship, if the grantor, beneficiary, or fiduciary materially participates in the operations or daily management of the business. Filing requirements would depend on this classification.

Unincorporated Business Organization (UBO)

A term used by trust promoters to identify trusts they sell and to disguise the fact that it is a trust. This term and the term "Massachusetts Business Trust" are often used interchangeably. These are not terms used by the Internal Revenue Code.

SAMPLE INDEPENDENT CONTRACTOR AGREEMENT

AGREEMENT made this _____ day of _____, 20_____, by and between
_____ (hereinafter "Corporation"), whose address
is _____ and
_____, whose address is _____
_____ (hereinafter "Contractor").

SERVICES TO BE PERFORMED

Contractor agrees to perform the following services for Corporation:

PLACE OF PERFORMANCE

The work described above shall be performed at:

TIME PERIOD

Contractor agrees to commence work as soon as practical and complete all work
by _____, 20_____. Contractor agrees to subtract $_____ per day for each
day the work is not completed as liquidated damages and not as a penalty from the total
bill of services performed.

PAYMENT FOR SERVICES

Contractor shall be paid as follows:

SUPERVISION

Corporation shall not supervise or directly control the work of Contractor. Corporation does reserve the right, from time to time, to inspect the work being performed
to determine whether it is being performed in a good and "workmanlike" manner. Contractor shall have the ultimate authority to determine the hours of work, the length of
workdays, the means and methods of performance of the work, and Corporation shall
not interfere in this regard.

MATERIALS

Contractor will obtain and provide all necessary materials for the services described above at his own expense.

INVOICES

Contractor agrees to provide Corporation with written invoices for all work performed.

SUBCONTRACTORS OR ASSISTANTS

Contractor may, in his discretion and at his own expense, employ such assistants or subcontractors as may be necessary for the performance of work. Contractor agrees to pay any wages, taxes, unemployment insurance, withholding taxes, workers' compensation insurance required by law for assistants or subcontractors. Said assistants or subcontractors will not be paid or supervised by Corporation.

EQUIPMENT

Contractor agrees to provide his own equipment or tools for the work to be performed.

INSURANCE

Contractor agrees to provide his own workers' compensation and liability insurance for work performed, naming Corporation as additional insured. In the event that Contractor does not maintain insurance, he shall defend and indemnify Corporation for all lawsuits, accidents, or claims arising out of his work, or the work of his assistants or subcontractors.

INDEPENDENT CONTRACTOR

Contractor agrees that he is completely independent from Corporation and is not an employee of Corporation. Contractor warrants that he may, and in fact does work for other individuals and/or entities.

_____   _____

Contractor   Corporation   by:

SAMPLE AGREEMENT TO CONVERT COMMUNITY PROPERTY

Agreement made this _____ day of _____, 20____, by and between _____ ("Husband") and ("Wife") of the County of _____, state of _____ .

WHEREAS, the parties have accumulated and acquired certain real and personal property subsequent to their marriage on the _____ day of _____, 20____, in the County of _____, State of _____, and

WHEREAS, all of the following property described in the annexed schedule "A" has been and is community property under the laws of the State of _____, and

WHEREAS, it is the intention of parties to convert the status of all of the above-described "community property" to separate property and hold the property as tenants in common with equal undivided interests therein,

THE PARTIES HEREBY AGREE AS FOLLOWS:

1. The parties agree to convey, by deed, all of the above property, heretofore held as community property, and to convey to each of them as tenants in common, within _____ days from the date of this agreement.

2. Each party agrees to execute and deliver to the other such bills of sale, deeds, and other documents and instruments necessary to convey the title to the property described in the annexed schedule "A" to each of them as tenants in common.

3. The parties expressly declare that the purpose and intent of this agreement is that each party is to acquire and own the property above referred to, in his or her individual right and as his or her sole and separate property, including the rents, issues, and profits therefrom, so that each may convey, transfer, assign, or otherwise transfer to his or her heirs at law, devisees, assignees, or legatees, without the interference or necessity of or by the other party consenting or signing any instruments in connection therewith.

4. Each of the parties agrees to waive all and every right whatsoever he or she might have or acquire by law in the community property of the marriage, whether now owned or hereafter to be acquired, and each party shall have sole control and management of, and the right to sell, convey, or transfer any and all of their properties trans-

ferred pursuant to this agreement, without signature or joining in by the other, to the extent permitted by the laws of the State of _____ respecting tenancy in common.

_____   _____
Husband   Wife

_____   _____
Witness   Witness

Sworn to before me this _____ day of _____, 20____, by _____ and _____, who personally appeared before me.

                                                    _____
                                                    Notary Public

SCHEDULE "A"
Community Property to be Converted

ITEM	DESCRIPTION	APPROX. VALUE

SAMPLE JOINT VENTURE AGREEMENT

AGREEMENT made and entered into this _____ day of _____, 20____, by and between _____, whose address is _____ (hereinafter referred to as the "First Party"), and _____, whose address is _____ (hereinafter referred to as the "Second Party"), and hereinafter collectively referred to as the "Venturers" or the "Parties."

WITNESSETH:

WHEREAS, it is the desire of the Parties to define and set out their relationship in writing and the circumstances under which they are operating, as of the date of this Agreement.

NOW, THEREFORE, in consideration of the mutual covenants hereinafter contained, the Venturers agree as follows:

PRIOR AGREEMENT. It is the intention of the Parties that this Agreement replace all oral agreements, understandings, and business ventures, previously, or otherwise, existing between the Parties.

PURPOSE. The purpose of the joint venture is to _____ _____ and to carry on any and all such other activities as may be necessary to the business of the joint venture.

TERM. The joint venture shall commence as of the day of the date of this agreement and shall continue until _____ or until terminated earlier by agreement of the parties or by operation of law.

LIABILITY OF THE PARTIES. During the existence of the joint venture, neither party shall be liable for any obligations of the other party created without the express approval of both parties. The Parties shall share equally in any and all profits and losses of the business of the joint venture.

REPRESENTATIONS AND WARRANTIES OF THE PARTIES. The Parties represent and warrant that there are no suits, judgments, or liens, of any kind, pending or filed against him/her, whether individually or in conjunction with any person or entity, in any jurisdiction whatsoever.

NATURE OF PERFORMANCE. During the experience of the joint venture, the Venturers shall be solely responsible for performing the following duties:

(a) The First Party shall

(b) The Second Party shall

JOINT VENTURE DECISIONS. All decisions, including, but not limited to, purchase of assets by the joint venture, any loan or other obligation to be undertaken by the joint venture, and the sale of any asset of the joint venture shall require the approval of all of the Venturers.

DISTRIBUTIONS. Distributions of any profits of the joint venture during the term of its existence shall be made at such times and in such amounts as the Venturers shall agree hereafter.

_____   _____
First Party   Second Party

SAMPLE LAND TRUST AGREEMENT

This land trust trust agreement, dated _____, 20____, is by and between
_____, as trustee, who is to take title to the
following described real estate in _____ County, State of _____,

[legal description]

to hold it for the uses and purposes and on the trusts set forth herein, and

the beneficiaries of this trust, who will be entitled to the earnings, avails, and proceeds
of the trust property according to the respective interests set forth herein.

1. Interests of beneficiaries as personalty. The interests of the beneficiaries will consist
solely of: (a) a power of direction to deal with title to the trust property, (b) a power to
manage and control the property as provided here, and (c) the right to receive the proceeds from rentals and from mortgages, sales, or other disposition of the property. The
right to the avails and proceeds of the property will be deemed to be personal property
and may be assigned and transferred as personal property.

The death of any beneficiary will not terminate the trust or in any manner affect the
powers of trustee. In case of the death of any beneficiary during the existence of this
trust, the beneficiary's interest will vest in the executor or administrator of the beneficiary's estate, and not to his or her heirs at law. No beneficiary now has or will have any
right, title, or interest in or to any proportion of any real estate, either legal or equitable,
but only an interest in the earnings, avails, and proceeds from it.

2. Assignment of beneficial interests. An assignment of a beneficial interest under this
agreement is binding on trustee until the trustee receives the original or a duplicate of
the assignment in a form satisfactory to trustee. Any assignment not so delivered to
trustee will be void as to all subsequent assignees or purchasers without notice.

3. Filing of income tax returns. Trustee will not be obligated to file any income, profit,
or other tax reports or schedules; the beneficiaries will individually make all such re-

ports, and pay any and all taxes on the earnings, avails, and proceeds of the trust property or growing out of their interest under this agreement.

4. Reimbursement and indemnification of trustee. If trustee makes any advances of money on account of this trust, is made a party to any litigation on account of holding title to the real estate or in connection with this trust, or is compelled to pay any sum of money on account of this trust, whether on account of breach of contract, injury to personal property, fines, or penalties under any law or otherwise, the beneficiaries will on demand pay to trustee all disbursements or advances or payments of this nature made by trustee, together with trustee's expenses, including reasonable attorneys' fees.

5. Protection of third parties dealing with trustee. No party dealing with trustee in relation to the trust property in any manner, and no party to whom the property or any part of it or interest in it is conveyed, contracted to be sold, leased, or mortgaged by trustee, will be obliged to see to the application of the purchase money paid or to inquire into the necessity or expediency of any act of trustee or the provisions of this instrument.

6. Trust agreement not to be recorded. This agreement will not be placed on record in the recorder's office of the county in which the trust property is situated, or elsewhere. This type of recording will not be considered notice of the rights of any person under this agreement derogatory to the title or powers of trustee.

7. Disclosure of names of beneficiaries. In the event of service of process on trustee at any time in the future, trustee may in its discretion disclose to the other parties to the proceeding the names and addresses of the beneficiary or beneficiaries. The trustee shall not divulge the identities of the beneficiaries under any other circumstances.

8. Duties of trustee. Trustee assumes and agrees to perform the following active and affirmative duties under this agreement, at the direction of the beneficiaries:

(a) Execution of instruments. The trustee shall execute the instruments necessary to protect and conserve the trust property; to sell, contract to sell, and grant options to purchase the property and any right, title, or interest on any terms; to exchange the property or any part for any other real or personal property on any terms; to convey the property by deed or other conveyance to any grantee, with or without consideration; to mortgage, execute principal and interest notes, pledge or otherwise encumber the property or any part; to lease, contract to lease, grant options to lease and renew, extend, amend, and otherwise modify leases on the property or any part, for any period of time, for any rental, and on any other terms and conditions; and to release, convey, or assign any other right, title, or interest whatsoever in the property or any part. All trust deeds, mortgages, and notes executed by trustee will contain provisions exempting and exonerating the beneficiaries under this trust from all personal obligation and liability whatsoever by reason of their execution and from any and all personal obligation or liability for the repayment of the borrowed money evidenced and secured by them. Trustee will not be required to inquire into the authenticity, necessity, or propriety of any written direction delivered to it pursuant to this paragraph or agreement. All trust deeds, mortgages, and notes executed by trustee may contain provisions exempting and exonerating trustee from all personal obligation and liability whatsoever by reason of their execution, and will contain provisions exempting and exonerating the beneficiary under this trust from all personal obligation and liability whatsoever by reason of their execution and from any and all personal obligation or liability for repayment of the borrowed money evidenced and secured by them.

(b) Sale of trust property and distribution of trust proceeds. If any property remains in trust under this agreement 20 years from the date here, trustee will sell the property at public sale after a reasonable public advertisement and reasonable notice of the sale to the beneficiaries. After deducting its reasonable fees and expenses, trustee will divide the proceeds of this sale among the beneficiaries as their interests may then appear without any direction or consent, or will transfer, set over, convey, and deliver to all the then beneficiaries of this trust their respective undivided interest in any nondivisible assets, or will transfer, set over, and deliver all of the assets of the trust to the beneficiaries in their respective proportionate interests at any time that the assets of the trust consist solely of cash.

8. Resignation of trustee. Trustee may resign at any time by sending a notice of its intention to do so by registered mail to each of the beneficiaries here at his or her address last known to trustee. This resignation will become effective 10 days after the mailing of the notices. In the event of this resignation, a successor or successors may be appointed by the person or persons then entitled to direct trustee in the disposition of the trust property, and trustee will then convey the trust property to the successor or successors in trust. If no successor in trust is named within ten days after the mailing of the notices, trustee may convey the trust property to the beneficiaries in accordance with their respective interests under this agreement, or trustee may, at its option, file a bill for appropriate relief in any court of competent jurisdiction. Notwithstanding this resignation, trustee will continue to have a first lien on the trust property for its costs, expenses, and attorneys' fees, and for its reasonable compensation. Every successor or successors in

trust will become fully vested with all the estate, properties, rights, powers, trusts, duties, and obligations of its, his, her, or their predecessor.

9. Beneficiaries to manage and operate trust property. The beneficiaries will, in their own right, have full and exclusive control over the management and operation of the trust property and control of the sale, rental, or other disposition. Each beneficiary, or his or her agent, will collect and otherwise handle his or her share of the rents and avails and the proceeds of any sale or other disposition. Trustee will have no duty respecting the payment of taxes, insurance premiums, or other costs or charges against or concerning the trust property.

10. Compensation of trustee. The beneficiaries will pay trustee as its compensation the following:

11. Successors bound. The terms and conditions of this agreement will inure to the benefit of and be binding on any successor trustee under this agreement, and on all successors in interest of the beneficiaries.

_____   _____

Trustee   Grantor/Beneficiary

_____   _____

Trustee   Grantor/Beneficiary

Sworn to and subscribed before me this _____ day of _____, 20____, by the parties named herein.

_____   [SEAL]

Notary Public

State of _____

SAMPLE LIVING TRUST AGREEMENT

DECLARATION OF TRUST, made as of this _____ day of _____, 20____, between _____ [NAME OF GRANTOR], having an address at _____, as grantor (hereinafter referred to as the "Grantor"), and _____ [NAME OF TRUSTEE], having an address as aforesaid, as trustee (hereinafter referred to as the 'Trustee").

WITNESSETH:

WHEREAS, the Grantor is the owner of the property more particularly described in Schedule A attached hereto and made a part hereof; and

WHEREAS, the Grantor's wife is _____ [WIFE'S NAME], and the Grantor has one child, [CHILD'S NAME]; and

WHEREAS, the Grantor desires to create a revocable trust of the property described in Schedule A hereto, together with such monies, securities, and other assets as the Trustee hereafter may hold or acquire hereunder (said property, monies, securities, and other assets, together with any additions thereto received pursuant to the Grantor's last will and testament or otherwise, being hereinafter referred to as the "trust estate"), for the purposes and upon the terms and conditions hereinafter set forth.

NOW, THEREFORE, in consideration of the covenants herein contained and other valuable consideration, the receipt and sufficiency of which hereby is acknowledged, the Grantor hereby transfers, conveys, assigns, and delivers to the Trustee as and for the trust estate the property more particularly described in Schedule A hereto, to hold the same, and any other property which the Trustee hereafter may acquire, IN TRUST, for the purposes and upon the terms and conditions hereinafter set forth:

ARTICLE FIRST
Directions of Grantor

The Trustee shall hold, manage, invest, and reinvest the trust estate, shall collect the income therefrom, and shall pay any part or all of the income and principal to whomever the Grantor from time to time may direct in writing.

Until the Grantor hereafter may direct to the contrary, the net income shall be paid to the Grantor quarter annually.

Any income not so paid or applied shall be accumulated and added to the principal of this trust at least quarter annually.

ARTICLE SECOND
Disability of Grantor

If at any time the Grantor, in the judgment of the successor Trustee, shall be under any legal disability or shall be unable to manage properly his affairs by reason of illness or mental or physical disability (whether or not a court of competent jurisdiction has declared the Grantor incompetent or mentally ill or has appointed a conservator or other legal representative for the Grantor), the successor Trustee may pay or apply so much or all of the net income and the principal of the trust estate as the successor Trustee deems necessary or advisable for the health, education, maintenance, or support of the Grantor, his wife, and his child, in such amounts and proportions as the successor Trustee may determine. The successor Trustee also may pay any gift taxes and income taxes incurred by the Grantor, whether caused by the sale of any assets comprising the trust estate or otherwise. Any income not so paid or applied shall be accumulated and added to the principal of this trust at least quarter annually.

In making any payment hereunder, the successor Trustee may consider, but shall not be required to consider, the income and other resources of the Grantor, his wife, and his child. No such payment shall be charged upon a subsequent division of the trust estate against the principal of any share which may be set apart for any beneficiary hereunder.

ARTICLE THIRD
Successor Beneficiaries

Upon the death of the Grantor, the Trustee shall hold, manage, invest, and reinvest the trust estate, shall collect the income therefrom, and shall pay the net income to or for the benefit of the Grantor's wife and child, for their health, education, maintenance, or support, in such amounts and proportions as the Trustee may deem advisable. In addition, the Trustee may pay to or for the benefit of the Grantor's wife and child, for their health, education, maintenance, or support, any part or all of the principal of this trust, as the Trustee may determine in the absolute discretion of the Trustee, without considering other resources available to the Grantor's wife and child. The Grantor's wife shall have the right to receive such portions of the principal of the trust as she from time to time may demand. Any commission payable with respect to the principal so withdrawn shall be charged against such principal.

Upon the death of the Grantor's wife, the remaining principal of the trust estate, together with any accrued and unpaid income thereon, shall be paid and distributed to the Grantor's then living issue, by representation.

If the Grantor's child shall then be under the age of twenty-one (21), this trust shall continue for the benefit of the child, in accordance with the aforesaid terms and conditions, until the child attains said age. At such time as the child shall attain the age of twenty-one (21) years, the trust for the child shall terminate and the balance of the principal thereof at that time remaining, together with any accrued and unpaid income thereon, shall be paid and distributed to the child, discharged of trust. If the child shall die prior to attaining the age of twenty-one (21) years, the principal of the child's trust at that time remaining, together with any accrued and unpaid income thereon, shall be paid and distributed to the then living issue of the child, by representation, or if there is no living issue of the Grantor, to those who would take from the child if the child had died without a will. If any such issue is the income beneficiary of another trust under this Agreement, any property which would pass to such issue shall instead be added to the principal of that trust.

If there are no issue of the Grantor then living, the trust estate shall be paid and distributed to such persons and in such proportions as the same would be distributed under the laws of the State of Colorado then in force had the Grantor then died intestate, a resident of Colorado, and the owner of said property.

ARTICLE FOURTH
Use of Principal

The Trustee is authorized, at any time and from time to time, to pay to, or apply to the use of, the beneficiary of any trust held hereunder, for such beneficiary's health, education, maintenance, or support, any part or all of the principal of such trust as the Trustee may determine in the absolute discretion of the Trustee, without necessarily taking into account other resources available to such beneficiary. No such payment shall be charged upon a subsequent division of the trust estate against the principal of any share which may be set apart for a beneficiary.

ARTICLE FIFTH
Rights to Demand Principal

The income beneficiary of any trust at any time held hereunder shall have the right to demand and receive from the principal of such trust in each of its fiscal years the greater of $5,000 or five (5) percent of the fair market value of such principal determined as of the date the request to withdraw is made by written notice to the Trustee. Such right shall lapse to the extent it is not exercised in any year. Any commission payable with respect to funds so withdrawn shall be charged against such funds.

ARTICLE SIXTH
Distributions to Minors or Incompetents

In any case in which the Trustee is authorized or directed by any provision of this Agreement to pay or distribute income or principal to any person who shall be a minor or incompetent, the Trustee, in the absolute discretion of the Trustee and without authorization of any court, may pay or distribute the whole or any part of such income or principal to such minor or incompetent personally, or may apply the whole or any part thereof directly to the health, education, maintenance, or support of such minor or incompetent, or may pay or distribute the whole or any part thereof to the guardian, committee, conservator, or other legal representative, wherever appointed, of such minor or incompetent or to the person with whom such minor or incompetent may from time to time reside, or in the case of a minor, may pay or distribute the whole or any part thereof to a custodian for such minor under any gifts to minors or transfers to minors act. Evidence of such payment or distribution or the receipt therefor by the person to whom any such payment of distribution is made shall be a full discharge of the Trustee from all liability with respect thereto, even though the Trustee may be such person.

The Trustee, in the absolute discretion of the Trustee, may defer payment or distribution of any or all income or principal to which a minor may be entitled until such minor shall attain the age of twenty-one (21) years, or to make such payment or distribution at any time and from time to time, during the minority of such minor, holding the whole or the undistributed portion thereof as a separate fund vested in such minor but subject to the power in trust hereby given to the Trustee to administer and invest such fund and to use the income or principal thereof for the benefit of such minor as if such fund were held in trust hereunder. No bond or other security and no periodic accounts shall be required with respect to such fund, and the same shall be subject to commission as if it were a separate trust fund. The Trustee shall pay and distribute any balance of such fund to such minor when such minor shall attain the age of twenty-one (21) years. Except as in hereinabove provided, if such minor shall die before attaining the age of twenty-one (21) years, the Trustee shall pay and distribute such balance to the personal representatives, executors, or administrators of the estate of such minor.

The word "minor" wherever used in this Article SIXTH, shall mean any person who has not attained the age of twenty-one (21) years.

ARTICLE SEVENTH
Payment of Debts

Upon the death of the Grantor, the Trustee may pay from the principal of the trust estate the amount of any estate or death taxes, by whatever name called, imposed under the laws of any jurisdiction by reason of the Grantor's death, whether in respect of property passing under this Agreement or the Grantor's last will and testament or otherwise, and the amount of all of the debts which the Grantor's estate must pay, the expenses of his last illnesses and funeral, and the expenses of administering his estate. The Trustee may rely upon the written certification of the personal representatives, executors, or administrators of Grantor's estate as to the amount of any such tax, debt, or expense, without any duty to inquire as to the correctness thereof, and, in its discretion, may make payment thereof either to said personal representatives, executors, or administrators or to the taxing authority or person to whom such amount is owed.

ARTICLE EIGHTH
Grantor's Right To Revoke Or Amend

The Grantor reserves the right, at any time and without the consent of any person or notice to any person other than the Trustee, to amend or revoke in whole or in part this Agreement or any trust created hereunder, including the right to change the terms or beneficiaries thereof, by delivering to the Trustee written notice of such amendment or revocation signed by the Grantor. No amendment of this Agreement, however, shall increase the obligations or reduce the commissions of the Trustee without the consent of the Trustee. Upon any such revocation, the Trustee shall deliver to the Grantor all property in the possession or control of the Trustee with respect to any trust which has been revoked and shall execute and deliver any instruments necessary to release any interest of the Trustee in such property. The sale or other disposition by the Grantor of the whole or any part of the trust estate held hereunder shall constitute as to such whole or part a revocation of this Agreement and the trust or trusts affected thereby.

The Grantor reserves the power and right during the life of the Grantor to collect any rent, interest, or other income which may accrue from the trust estate and, in his sole discretion, to accumulate such income as a trust asset or to pay such income to the Grantor individually and not in any fiduciary capacity. The Grantor further reserves the power and right during the life of the Grantor to mortgage or pledge all or any part of the trust estate as collateral for any loan.

ARTICLE NINTH
Powers of Trustee

In the administration of any property, real or personal, at any time forming a part of the trust estate, including accumulated income, and in the administration of any trust created hereunder, the Trustee, in addition to and without limitation of the powers provided by law, shall have the following powers to be exercised in the absolute discretion of the Trustee, except as otherwise expressly provided in this Agreement:

(a) To retain such property for any period, whether or not the same is of the character permissible for investments by fiduciaries under any applicable law, and without regard to the effect any such retention may have upon the diversity of investments:

(b) To sell, transfer, exchange, convert, or otherwise dispose of, or grant options with respect to, such property, at public or private sale, with or without security, in such manner, at such times, for such prices, and upon such terms and conditions as the Trustee may deem advisable;

(c) To invest and reinvest in common or preferred stocks, securities, investment trusts, bonds and other property, real or personal, foreign or domestic, including any undivided interest in any one or more common trust funds, whether or not such investments be of the character permissible for investments by fiduciaries under any applicable law, and without regard to the effect any such investment may have upon the diversity of investments;

(d) To render liquid the trust estate or any trust created hereunder in whole or in part, at any time and from time to time, and to hold unproductive property, cash, or readily marketable securities of little or no yield for such period as the Trustee may deem advisable;

(e) To lease any such property beyond the period fixed by statute for leases made by fiduciaries and beyond the duration of any trust created hereunder.

(f) To join or become a party to, or to oppose, any reorganization, readjustment, recapitalization, foreclosure, merger, voting trust, dissolution, consolidation, or exchange, and to deposit any securities with any committee, depository, or trustee, and to pay any fees, expenses, and assessments incurred in connection therewith, and to charge the same to principal, and to exercise conversion, subscription, or other rights, and to make any necessary payments in connection therewith, or to sell any such privileges;

(g) To vote in person at meetings of stock or security holders and adjournments thereof, and to vote by general or limited proxy with respect to any stock securities;

(h) To hold stock and securities in the name of a nominee without indicating the trust character of such holding, or unregistered or in such form as will pass by delivery, or to use a central depository and to permit registration in the name of a nominee.

(i) To initiate or defend, at the expense of the trust estate, any litigation relating to this Agreement or any property of the trust estate which the Trustee considers advisable, and to pay, compromise, compound, adjust, submit to arbitration, sell, or release any claims or demands of the trust estate or any trust created hereunder against others or of others against the same as the Trustee may deem advisable, including the acceptance of deeds of real property in satisfaction of notes, bonds, and mortgages, and to make any payments in connection therewith which the Trustee may deem advisable;

(j) To borrow money for any purpose from any source, including any trustee at any time acting hereunder, and to secure the repayment of any and all amounts so borrowed by mortgage or pledge of any property;

(k) To possess, manage, develop, subdivide, control, partition, mortgage, lease, or otherwise deal with any and all real property; to satisfy and discharge or extend the term of any mortgage, deed of trust or similar instrument thereof; to execute the necessary instruments and covenants to effectuate the foregoing powers, including the giving or granting of options in connection therewith; to make repairs, replacements, and improvements, structural or otherwise, or abandon the same if deemed to be worthless or not of sufficient value to warrant keeping or protecting; to abstain from the payment of real estate taxes, assessments, water charges and sewer rents, repairs, maintenance and upkeep of the same; to permit to be lost by tax sale or other proceeding or to convey the same for a nominal consideration or without consideration; to set up appropriate reserves out of income for repairs, modernization, and upkeep of buildings, including reserves for depreciation and obsolescence, and to add such reserves to principal and, if the income from the property itself should not suffice for such purposes, to advance out of other income any sums needed therefore, and advance any income of the trust for the amortization of any mortgage, deed of trust, or similar instrument on property held in the trust;

(l) To purchase from the legal representatives of the estate of the Grantor (or the estate of the Grantor's wife) or from the trustees of any trust established by the Grantor (or by the Grantor's wife) any property constituting a part of such estate or trust at its fair market value and to make loans for adequate consideration to such legal representatives or trustees, upon such terms and conditions as the Trustee may determine in the absolute discretion of the Trustee;

(m) To carry insurance of the kinds and in the amounts which the Trustee considers advisable, at the expense of the trust estate, to protect the trust estate and the Trustee and personally against any hazard;

(n) To make distribution of the trust estate or of the principal of any trust created hereunder in cash or in kind, or partly in kind, and to cause any distribution to be composed of cash, property, or undivided fractional shares in property different in kind from any other distribution, and to determine the fair valuation of the property so allocated, with or without regard to the tax basis; to hold the principal of separate trusts in a consolidated fund and to invest the same as a single fund; to split trusts for purposes of allocating GST exemptions (within the meaning of Section 2642(a) of the Internal Revenue Code); and to merge any trusts which have substantially identical terms and beneficiaries, and to hold them as a single trust;

(o) To employ and pay the compensation of accountants, attorneys, experts, investment counselors, custodians, agents, and other persons, or firms providing services or advice, irrespective of whether the Trustee may be associated therewith; to delegate discretionary powers to such persons or firms; and to rely upon information or advice furnished thereby or to ignore the same, as the Trustee in its discretion may determine;

(p) To execute and deliver any and all instruments or writings which may deem advisable to carry out any of the foregoing powers; and

(q) To exercise all such rights and powers and to do all such acts and enter into all such agreements as persons owning similar property in their own right might lawfully exercise, do, or enter into.

Except as otherwise provided herein, the Trustee may determine, when there is reasonable doubt or uncertainty as to the applicable law or the relevant facts, which receipts of money or other assets should be credited to income or principal, and which disbursements, commissions, assessments, fees, and other expenses should be charged to income or principal. Any distributions or dividends payable in the stock of a corporation, and rights to subscribe to securities or rights other than cash declared or issued by a corporation, shall be dealt with as principal. The proceeds from the sale, redemption, or other disposition, whether at a profit or loss, and regardless of the tax treatment thereof, of any property constituting principal, including mortgages or similar instruments and real estate acquired through foreclosure or otherwise, shall normally be dealt with as principal, but the Trustee may allocate a portion of any such proceeds to income if the property disposed of produced no income or substantially less than the current rate of return on trust investments, or if the Trustee shall deem such action advisable for any other reason. The preceding provisions of this paragraph shall not be deemed to authorize any act by the Trustee which may be a violation of any law prohibiting the accumulation of income.

No person who deals with any Trustee hereunder shall be bound to see to the application of any asset delivered to such Trustee or to inquire into the authority for, or propriety of, any action taken or not taken by such Trustee.

Notwithstanding anything to the contrary contained herein, during such time as any current or possible future beneficiary of any trust created hereunder (other than the Grantor) may be acting as a Trustee hereunder, such person shall be disqualified from exercising any power to make any discretionary distributions of income or principal to himself or herself (unless the discretion to make such distributions is limited by an ascertainable standard within the meaning of Section 2041(b)(1)(A) of the Internal Revenue Code), or to satisfy any of his or her legal obligations, or to make discretionary allocations of receipts or disbursements as between income and principal. No Trustee who is a current or possible future beneficiary of any trust hereunder (other than the Grantor) shall participate in the exercise of any powers of the Trustee which would cause such beneficiary to be treated as the owner of trust assets for tax purposes.

No Trustee shall be liable for acts or omission in administering the trust estate or any trust created by this Agreement, except for that Trustee's own actual fraud, gross negligence, or willful misconduct. If any Trustee becomes liable as Trustee to any other person who is not a beneficiary in connection with any matter not within the Trustee's control and not due to the Trustee's actual fraud, gross negligence, or willful misconduct, such Trustee shall be fully indemnified and held harmless by the trust estate and any trust created hereunder giving rise to such liability, as the case may be, against and in respect of any damages that such Trustee may sustain, including without limitation attorneys' fees. No successor Trustee shall incur any liability, by reason of qualifying as a Trustee hereunder, for the acts or omissions of any predecessor Trustee.

The Trustee is authorized, but not required, to accept any property transferred to the Trustee by any person during such person's lifetime or by such person's last will and testament. Any property so transferred to, and accepted by, the Trustee shall become a part of such trust or trusts created by this Agreement as such person shall direct and may be commingled with the other property in the trust or trusts to which said property has been added and held, administered, and disposed of as a part of such trust or trusts.

ARTICLE TENTH
Appointment Of Trustee

The Grantor appoints himself as Trustee hereunder. The Grantor hereby appoints _____ [NAME OF SUCCESSOR TRUSTEE], having an address at _____, as successor Trustee hereunder in the event of the death of the Grantor, or his physical or mental incapacity.

The term "Trustee" wherever used herein shall mean the trustee in office from time to time. Any such trustee shall have the same rights, powers, duties, authority, and privileges, whether or not discretionary, as if originally appointed hereunder.

No bond, surety, or other security shall be required of any Trustee acting hereunder for the faithful performance of the duties of Trustee, notwithstanding any law of any State or other jurisdiction to the contrary.

ARTICLE ELEVENTH
Accounts Of Trustee

The Trustee, at any time and from time to time, may render to the Grantor an account of the acts and transactions of the Trustee with respect to the income and principal of any trust created hereunder, from the date of the creation of such trust or from the date of the last previous account of the Trustee. After the death of the Grantor, the Trustee, at any time and from time to time, may render an account to the living person or persons who are entitled, at the time of such account, to receive all or a portion of the income of the trusts herein created. The approval of any person of full age, or a guardian or parent of a minor or incompetent person, to whom an account is rendered shall, as to all matters stated therein, be final and binding upon him or such minor or incompetent person, or any persons claiming through him or such minor or incompetent person, as the case may be. A person of full age, or a guardian or parent of a minor or incompetent person, to whom an account is rendered shall be deemed to have approved the account if he assents to the account in writing or if he does not communicate to the Trustee his written objections to the account within sixty (60) days after the receipt of the account (provided the account was accompanied by a notice of said sixty (60)-day period within to raise objections.

The Grantor shall have full power and authority on behalf of all persons interested in any trust hereunder, whether such interest relates to income or principal, to settle any account of the Trustee. Such settlement shall be final and binding upon all persons so interested in such trust. Upon such settlement, the Trustee shall be fully and completely discharged and released from all further liability with respect to acts and transactions set forth in the account so settled.

The Trustee shall not be required at any time to file any account in any court, nor shall the Trustee be required to have any account judicially settled. Nothing herein, however, shall be construed as limiting the right of the Trustee to seek a judicial settlement of any account.

ARTICLE THIRTEENTH
Simultaneous Death

If any beneficiary under this Agreement shall die simultaneously with the Grantor or any other person upon whose death such beneficiary shall become entitled to receive either income or principal under this Agreement, or in such circumstances as to render it difficult or impracticable to determine who predeceased the other, then for purposes of this Agreement such beneficiary shall be deemed to have predeceased the Grantor or such other person. The provisions of this Agreement shall be construed as aforesaid, notwithstanding the provisions of any applicable law establishing a different presumption of order of death or providing for survivorship for a fixed period as a condition of inheritance of property.

ARTICLE FOURTEENTH
Rights of Beneficiaries Are Not Assignable

No disposition, charge, or encumbrance on the income or principal of any trust established hereunder shall be valid or binding upon the Trustee. No beneficiary shall have any right, power, or authority to assign, transfer, encumber, or otherwise dispose of such income or principal or any part thereof until the same shall be paid to such beneficiary by the Trustee. No income or principal shall be subject in any manner to any claim of any creditor of any beneficiary or liable to attachment, execution, or other process of law prior to its actual receipt by the beneficiary.

ARTICLE FIFTEENTH
Construction

The validity and construction of this Agreement and the trusts created hereunder shall be governed by the laws of the State of Colorado.

Any provision herein which refers to a statute, rule, regulation, or other specific legal reference which is no longer in effect at the time said provision is to be applied shall be deemed to refer to the successor, replacement, or amendment to such statute, rule, regulation, or other reference, if any, and shall be interpreted in such a manner so as to carry out the original intent of said provision.

For purposes of this Agreement, the disability or incapacity of an individual (including the Grantor or any Trustee) shall be conclusively established by a written statement signed by such individual's then attending physician and filed with the records of any trust established hereunder attesting that, in such physician's opinion, such individual is unable to manage his or her affairs. Such written statement shall be conclusive evidence of such fact, and any third party may rely on same in dealing with any trust established hereunder and shall not be obliged to inquire whether such individual is no longer under such disability or incapacity at the time of such dealings.

Wherever used in this Agreement and the context so requires, the masculine shall include the feminine and the singular shall include the plural, and vice versa.

The captions in this Agreement are for convenience of reference, and they shall be considered when construing this Agreement.

If under any of the provisions of this Agreement any portion of the trust estate would be held in trust beyond a date twenty-one (21) years after the death of the last survivor of the Grantor, his wife, and the issue of the Grantor and other beneficiaries hereunder in being when this Agreement becomes irrevocable; then, upon such date, the trust of such portion shall terminate and the principal, and any unpaid income thereof, shall be paid and distributed to the person or persons then living who would have been entitled to receive the income therefrom had the trust continued, in the proportions to which they would have been entitled.

ARTICLE SIXTEENTH
Binding Effect

This agreement shall extend to and be binding upon the heirs, personal representatives, executors, administrators, successors, and assigns of the undersigned Grantor and upon the Trustee acting hereunder.

ARTICLE SEVENTEENTH
Short Name

This Agreement and the trusts created hereunder may be referred to, in any other instrument by the name: "_____ Living Trust dated _____, 20____." Any transfers to this Agreement or any trust hereunder may refer to the aforesaid name or to "_____ as Trustee under _____ Living Trust dated _____, 20____," with or without specifying any change in Trustee or any amendment to this Agreement.

IN WITNESS WHEREOF, this Agreement has been duly executed as of the date first above written.

_____
NAME OF GRANTOR
Grantor

STATE OF   )
COUNTY OF   ) SS.:

The foregoing instrument was acknowledged before me on the _____ day of 20____, by _____ [NAME OF GRANTOR].

IN WITNESS WHEREOF I hereunto set my hand and official seal.

_____
Notary Public
My commission expires on

SCHEDULE A

TRUST ESTATE PROPERTY

SAMPLE FAMILY LIMITED PARTNERSHIP AGREEMENT

THIS AGREEMENT is made and entered into this _____ day of _____, 20____, by and between the General Partners whose names and addresses are set out in Schedule 1, attached hereto (hereinafter referred to as the "General Partners"), and the Limited Partners whose names and addresses are set out in Schedule 2, attached hereto (hereinafter referred to as the "Limited Partners").

1. Name and Business. The name of the partnership shall be _____ FAMILY LIMITED PARTNERSHIP (referred to as the "Partnership"), and the principal office and place of business of the Partnership shall be at _____ _____. The parties hereby form a Limited Partnership pursuant to the provisions of the Partnership Laws of the State of _____ for the purpose of investing in real estate, stocks, securities, mutual funds, or any such business that may be lawful under the Limited Partnership Act of the State of _____ _____. The Partnership may enter into any other investments, ventures, and business arrangements deemed prudent by the General Partners in order to achieve successful operations for the Partnership.

2. Term. The term of the Partnership shall begin on _____, 20____, and shall continue for a period of 35 years unless terminated earlier as hereinafter provided.

3. Contributions of General Partners. The General Partners shall contribute to the Partnership capital the cash amount or other consideration set opposite their names in the attached Exhibit "A."

4. Capital Contributions of Limited Partners. The Limited Partners shall contribute to the Partnership the consideration capital the cash amounts set opposite their names in the attached Exhibit "B."

5. Salaries, Drawings, and Interest on Capital Contributions. The General Partners shall receive the salaries as set out in Exhibit "D" which are determined to be reasonable compensation for services rendered the Partnership. Such salaries shall be paid prior to any distribution of net profits to the partners. The Limited Partners shall receive no salaries or any other compensation for services rendered the Partnership. No partner shall receive draws for services rendered on behalf of the Partnership in their capacity as partners, nor shall any partner receive any interest on his or her contribution to the capital of the Partnership.

6. Profits and Losses.

a. The net profits and losses of the Partnership shall be divided and borne by each of the partners in the proportion to which the partners contributed capital. Such distribution of net profits shall be subsequent and without regard to salaries provisioned for in paragraph 5, subject, however, insofar as the Limited Partners are concerned, to the limitation of their liability to the amount of their individual investment, as therein provided. **NOTWITHSTANDING ANYTHING TO THE CONTRARY HEREIN, NO DISTRIBUTIONS WILL BE MADE TO THE LIMITED PARTNERS WITHOUT THE CONSENT OF THE GENERAL PARTNERS. THE GENERAL PARTNERS' DECISION AND DISCRETION SHALL BE FINAL IN THIS REGARD.**

b. The fiscal year of the Partnership shall be the calendar year.

7. Sale of Assets. If any asset held by the Partnership is sold, the net proceeds realized from such sale shall be allocated in the proportion as follows:

a. Each partner shall receive an amount equal to the cash contributions made to the original capital of the Partnership as set forth in paragraphs 3 and 4 hereof.

b. The next **ONE** (1%) percent, after the allocations set forth in subparagraph (a) of this paragraph shall be divided among the General Partners in the proportions as stated in paragraph 3 hereof and NINETY-NINE (99%) PERCENT among the Limited Partners in the proportions to which their capital contributions set forth in paragraph 4 hereof bear to each other, or as the General and Limited Partners may agree. **NOTWITHSTANDING ANYTHING TO THE CONTRARY HEREIN, NO DISTRIBUTIONS WILL BE MADE TO THE LIMITED PARTNERS WITHOUT THE CONSENT OF THE GENERAL PARTNERS. THE GENERAL PARTNERS' DECISION AND DISCRETION SHALL BE FINAL IN THIS REGARD.**

8. Losses. The liability of any of the Limited Partners for Partnership losses shall in no event exceed the aggregate amount of his or her contribution to the capital of the Partnership. Any losses in excess of such amount shall be borne solely by the General Partners, who shall share such losses in the proportions set forth herein.

9. Management, Duties, and Restrictions.

a. General Partners. All General Partners are deemed to be of sufficient maturity and experience to understand and take part in active management of the Partnership. The General Partners shall have equal rights in the management of the Partnership business and each shall devote such time to the Partnership as shall be reasonably required for its welfare and success. No General Partner shall do any act detrimental to the best interests of the Partnership.

b. Limited Partners. No Limited Partner shall participate in the management of the Partnership business. A Limited Partner shall have the right to withdraw his or her capital contribution upon the termination of the Partnership as provided herein; provided, however, that no part of the capital contribution of any Limited Partner shall be withdrawn unless all liabilities of the Partnership, except liabilities to partners on account of their contributions, have been paid or unless the Partnership has assets sufficient to pay them. No Limited Partner shall have the right to demand or receive property other than cash in return for his or her contribution. No Limited Partner shall have priority over any other Limited Partner either as to contributions to capital or as to compensation by way of income. The Limited Partners consent to any decisions made on behalf of the Partnership by General Partners in their capacity as managers thereof.

10. Banking. All funds of the Partnership shall be deposited in its name in such checking account or accounts as shall be designated by the General Partners. All withdrawals therefrom are to be made upon checks jointly signed by the General Partners, the survivor of them, or by the General Partner or Agent designated by all the General Partners.

11. Conveyance. Any deed, bill of sale, mortgage, security agreement, lease, contract for sale and purchase, or other commitment purporting to convey or encumber the interest of the Partnership in all or any portion of any real or personal property, shall be jointly signed by the General Partners, or by the survivor of them.

12. Books. The Partnership shall maintain full and accurate books in its principal office, or such other place as shall be designated for such purpose by the General Partners, and all partners shall have the right to inspect and examine such books at reasonable times. The books shall be closed and balanced at the end of each fiscal year.

13. Sale, Assignment, or Transfer of Interest. No partner shall sell or assign his or her interest in the partnership without the prior written consent of all other partners or

their guardian. Any sale or assignment by a partner shall be to parent, spouse, children, or trustee unless otherwise agreed to in writing between the other limited partners.

14. Death, Retirement, or Insanity of a General Partner. Should a General Partner die, retire, divorce, become insane, or have a lawsuit entered against them or in any way become financially insolvent or distressed (as determined in the sole discretion by a majority of the limited partners), that Partner's interest shall be terminated immediately and said General Partner's interest in the Partnership shall be liquidated from the partnership funds, if available, in cash, in the amount of his initial capital contribution or in the amount equal to his pro-rata share of the partnership's assets, whichever is greater. If the amount is greater than $1,000.00, the partnership shall execute a promissory note for the balance owed for a term of not less than five years bearing an annual interest rate of eight percent (8%). The Limited Partners reserve the right to appoint a new General Partner in his place upon a majority vote of the Limited Partners.

15. Death of a Limited Partner. The death of a Limited Partner shall not dissolve the Partnership or terminate the Partnership business.

16. Disclosure. The General Partners agree not to disclose the identity of the limited partners unless so ordered by a court of competent jurisdiction.

17. Termination. The Partnership may be terminated by agreement of the General Partners prior to the end of its term, after at least 30 days' prior written notice by the General Partners to each of the Limited Partners. In such event, the General Partners shall wind up and liquidate the Partnership by either or both of the following methods:

a. Selling the Partnership's assets and distributing the net proceeds therefrom after the payment of Partnership liabilities to each partner in satisfaction of his or her interest in the Partnership.

b. Distributing the Partnership's assets to the Partners in kind, each Partner accepting an undivided interest in the Partnership's assets, subject to its liabilities, in satisfaction of his or her interest in the Partnership. Upon completion of the liquidation, the Partnership shall be deemed completely dissolved and terminated.

18. Distribution of Proceeds on Liquidation. The proceeds of liquidation shall be distributed, as realized, in payment of the liabilities of the Partnership in the following order: (a) to creditors of the Partnership; (b) to all of the Partners in respect of their cap-

ital accounts as determined pursuant to the provisions of this Agreement. The General Partners shall not be personally liable to the Limited Partners for any deficit in the Limited Partners' capital accounts or for the return of their contributions. In the event of a liquidating distribution of the Partnership's property in kind, the fair market value of such property shall be determined by an appraiser agreeable to the Partners and each Partner shall receive an undivided interest in such property equal to the portion of capital contributed.

19. Power of Attorney. Each of the Limited Partners constitutes and appoints the General Partners the true and lawful attorney for the undersigned, to make, execute, sign, acknowledge, and file a Certificate of Limited Partnership or amendments thereto, and, upon termination of the Partnership, a Certificate of Dissolution, as required under the laws of this state, and also to make, execute, sign, acknowledge, and file such other instruments as may be required under the laws of this state. The General Partners are authorized to take title to the real property herein referred to and to execute any and all documents related thereto on behalf of the Partnership, whether or not a Certificate of Limited Partnership has been filed prior to the date of such acceptance of title or execution of such documents, and all of the parties hereto hereby ratify and confirm any such action by the General Partners. The aforementioned General Partners shall convey the real property, herein before referred to, to the Partnership upon the filing of a Certificate of Limited Partnership and the completion of any advertising and/or other requirements of the laws of this state.

20. Liability of General Partners. The General Partners shall not be liable for any action taken or omitted, which may result in loss or damage to the Partnership, if such action was taken or omitted in reliance upon the opinion of legal or other professional counsel for the Partnership.

21. Notices. All notices provided for in this Agreement shall be directed to the parties at the addresses hereinabove set forth and to the Partnership at its principal office by registered or certified mail.

22. Binding Effect. This Agreement shall be binding upon all the parties and their estates, heirs, or legatees.

23. Governing Law. This agreement, and all transactions contemplated hereby, shall be governed by, construed, and enforced in accordance with the laws of the State of _____.

24. Agreement in Counterparts. This Agreement may be executed in several counterparts, all of which shall constitute one agreement, binding on all the parties hereto, notwithstanding that all the parties are not signatory to the original or the same counterpart.

IN WITNESS WHEREOF, the parties have hereunto set their hands and seals on the day and year first above written.

Signed, sealed, and delivered in the presence of:

"GENERAL PARTNERS":

_____   _____

"LIMITED PARTNERS":

_____   _____

SAMPLE LIMITED LIABILITY COMPANY
OPERATING AGREEMENT (SHORT FORM)

Limited Liability Company Agreement ("Agreement") entered into this _____ day of _____, 20____, by and between _____ (the "Company") and _____ _____ (the "Members").

The Members hereby form a limited liability company pursuant to and in accordance with the Limited Liability Company Act of the state of _____ (the "Act"). In consideration of the mutual covenants and conditions herein, the Members agree as follows:

1. Name. The name of the limited liability company formed hereby is _____ _____.

2. Purpose. The Company is formed for the object and purpose of, and the nature of the business to be conducted and promoted by the Company is, engaging in any lawful act or activity for which limited liability companies may be formed under the Act and engaging in any and all activities necessary or incidental to the foregoing.

3. Registered Office. The address of the registered office of the Company in the State of _____ is _____.

4. Registered Agent. The name and address of the registered agent of the Company for service of process on the Company in the State of _____ is _____.

5. Members. The names and the business, residence, or mailing addresses of the Members are as follows:

_____

_____

_____

_____

6. Powers. The business and affairs of the Company shall be managed by the Members. The Members shall have the power to do any and all acts necessary or convenient to or for the furtherance of the purposes described herein, including all powers, statutory or otherwise, possessed by members under the laws of the State of _____.

7. Dissolution. The Company shall dissolve, and its affairs shall be wound up upon the first to occur of the following: (a) the written consent of the Members, (b) the death, retirement, resignation, expulsion, bankruptcy, or dissolution of a Member, (c) the entry of a decree of judicial dissolution under §18-802 of the Act, or (d) the termination date of the Company as provided in the Articles of Organization.

8. Capital Contributions. The Members have contributed the following amounts, in cash, and no other property, to the Company as defined in the annexed schedule "A." No Member is required to make any additional capital contribution to the Company.

9. Allocation of Profits and Losses. The Company's profits and losses shall be allocated in proportion to the initial capital contributions of the Members.

10. Distributions. Distributions shall be made to the Members at the times and in the aggregate amounts determined by the Members. Such distributions shall be allocated among the Members in the same proportion as their capital account balances.

11. Assignments. A Member may not assign in whole or in part his limited liability company interest without the express written permission of the other members, who shall have the first right of refusal to purchase said interest for a period of 60 days. Any assignment of membership interest shall be economic rights only and not make the assignee a member or give such assignee voting or participation rights in the Company.

12. Liability of Members. The Members shall not have any liability for the obligations or liabilities of the Company except to the extent provided in the Act.

IN WITNESS WHEREOF, this Limited Liability Company Operating Agreement has been duly executed by or on behalf of the parties hereto as of the date first above written.

_____   _____
MEMBER   MEMBER

_____   _____
MEMBER   MEMBER

State of Nevada

Office of the Secretary of State

Domestic Corporations
Filing Packet

Compiled By:
Commercial Recordings Division of
Dean Heller
Secretary of State

202 N. Carson Street
Carson City, NV 89701-4201
(775)684-5708

555 E. Washington Avenue, #4000
Las Vegas, NV 89101
(702)486-2880

DEAN HELLER
Secretary of State

202 North Carson Street
Carson City, Nevada 89701-4201
(775) 684 5708

Articles of
Incorporation
(PURSUANT TO NRS 78)

Office Use Only:

Important: Read attached instructions before completing form.

1. *Name of Corporation:*	
2. *Resident Agent Name and Street Address:* *(must be a Nevada address where process may be served)*	Name _____, **NEVADA** _____ Street Address City Zip Code Optional Mailing Address City State Zip Code
3. *Shares:* *(number of shares corporation authorized to issue)*	Number of shares with par value: _____ Par value: $_____ Number of shares without par value: _____
4. *Names, Addresses, Number of Board of Directors/Trustees:*	The First Board of Directors/Trustees shall consist of _____ members whose names and addresses are as follows: 1._____ Name _____, _____ _____ Street Address City State Zip Code 2._____ Name _____, _____ _____ Street Address City State Zip Code 3._____ Name _____, _____ _____ Street Address City State Zip Code 4._____ Name _____, _____ _____ Street Address City State Zip Code
5. *Purpose:* *(optional-see instructions)*	The purpose of this Corporation shall be:
6. *Other Matters:* *(see instructions)*	Number of additional pages attached: _____
7. *Names, Addresses and Signatures of Incorporators:* *(attach additional pages if there are more than 2 incorporators).*	Name Signature Address City State Zip Code Name Signature Address City State Zip Code
8. *Certificate of Acceptance of Appointment of Resident Agent:*	I hereby accept appointment as Resident Agent for the above named corporation. _____ _____ Authorized Signature of R.A. or On Behalf of R.A. Company Date

This form must be accompanied by appropriate fees. See attached fee schedule.

Nevada Secretary of State Form CORPART1999.01
Revised on: 12/19/02

DEAN HELLER
Secretary of State

202 North Carson Street
Carson City, Nevada 89701-4201
(775) 684 5708

Instructions for
Articles of Incorporation
(PURSUANT TO NRS 78)

IMPORTANT: READ ALL INSTRUCTIONS CAREFULLY BEFORE COMPLETING FORM.

1.   *Name of the Corporation.*   A name appearing to be that of a natural person and containing a given name or initials must not be used as a corporate name except with the addition of a corporate ending such as Incorporated, Inc., Limited, Ltd., Company, Co., Corporation, Corp. or other words that identifies it as not being a natural person. The name must be distinguishable from the names of corporations, limited-liability companies, limited partnerships, business trusts or limited-liability partnerships on file in the office of the Secretary of State. A name may be reserved, if available, for 90 days by submitting a written request with a $20.00 filing fee.

2.   *Resident Agent.* Persons wishing to incorporate in the State of Nevada must designate a person as a resident agent who resides or is located in this state. Every resident agent must have a street address in this state for the service of process, and may have a separate mailing address such as a post office box, which may be different from the street address.

3.   State the number of shares the corporation shall have the authority to issue with par value and its par value in appropriate space provided. State the number of shares without par value in the space provided for shares without par value.

4.   Indicate the number of members of the first board. State the names and addresses of the first governing board. Use a separate 8$\frac{1}{2}$ x 11 sheet as necessary for additional members. Directors or trustees must be at least 18 year of age.

5.   This section is optional and is required only if the corporation is to engage in insurance or banking. Pre-approval from the State Insurance Commissioner or the State Financial Institutions Division is necessary if you have either of these purposes.

6.   On a separate 8$\frac{1}{2}$ x 11, white sheet you may state additional information you wish to be part of the articles. This is an optional provision. If the additional information is contradictory to information on the form, the entire filing will be returned for correction.

7.   Names and addresses of the incorporators are required. Each incorporator must sign. Additional 8$\frac{1}{2}$ x 11 white sheet will be necessary if more than 2 incorporators.

8.   Resident agent must complete and sign certificate of acceptance at bottom of form or attach a separate signed certificate of acceptance.

IMPORTANT

INITIAL LIST OF OFFICERS: Pursuant to NRS 78.150, each corporation organized under the laws of this state shall, on or before the first day of the second month after the filing of its articles of incorporation, and annually thereafter, file its list of officers, directors and resident agent. The initial list fee is $165.00, thereafter, $85.00 per year. Forms will be mailed to you upon the organization of your corporation and annually thereafter to the corporationis resident agent.

COPIES: You *must* send in the number of copies you would like certified and returned to you in addition to the original article to be filed. A filing fee of $20.00 for each certification is required. Copies received without the required fee shall be returned uncertified. NRS 78.105 requires that a corporation receive at least one certified copy to be kept in the office of the resident agent. The Secretary of State keeps the original filing.

FILING FEE: Filing fee is based on the number of shares authorized. Please see the attached fee schedule. Filing may be expedited for an additional $100.00 expedite fee.

Filing may be submitted at the office of the Secretary of State or by mail at the following addresses:

(Regular and Expedited Filings Accepted)	(Expedited Filings Only)
Secretary of State	Secretary of State-Satellite Office
New Filings Division	Commercial Recordings Division
202 N. Carson Street	555 E. Washington Avenue, Suite 4000
Carson City, NV 89701-4201	Las Vegas, NV 89101
775-684-5708 Fax 775-684-5725	702-486-2880 Fax 702-486-2888

State of Nevada
Secretary of State
202 North Carson Street
Carson City, Nevada 89701-4201

Phone: (775) 684 5708

> ## Profit Corporation Fee Schedule
> ## Effective 8-1-01

PROFIT CORPORATIONS INITIAL FILING FEE : Pursuant to NRS 78, 80, 78A, and 89
Domestic and Foreign Corporations, Close Corporations and Professional Corporations.

Fees are based on the value of the total number of authorized shares stated in the Articles of Incorporation:

$75,000 or less	$175.00
$75,001 and not over $200,000	$225.00
$200,001 and not over $500,000	$325.00
$500,001 and not over $1,000,000	$425.00
OVER $1,000,000	
For the first $1,000,000	$425.00
For each additional $500,000 - or fraction thereof	$225.00
Maximum fee	$25,000.00

For the purpose of computing the filing fee, the value (capital) represented by the total number of shares authorized in the Articles of Incorporation is determined by computing the:

A. total authorized shares multiplied by their par value or;
B. total authorized shares without par value multiplied by $1.00 or;
C. the sum of (a) and (b) above if both par and no par shares.

Filing fees are calculated on a minimum par value of one-tenth of a cent (.001), regardless if the stated par value is less.

The 24 hour expedite fee for Articles of Incorporation for any of the above entities is $100.00 in addition to the filing fee based upon stock.

The 2 hour expedite fee is $500.00 in addition to the filing fee based upon stock.

PLEASE NOTE: the expedite fee is in addition to the standard filing fee charged on each filing and/or order.

24 HOUR EXPEDITE TIME CONSTRAINTS:

Each filing submitted receives same day filing date and may be picked up within 24 hours. Filings to be mailed out no later than the next business day following receipt.

Expedite period begins when filing or service request is received in this office in fileable form.

The Secretary of State reserves the right to extend the expedite period in times of extreme volume, staff shortages, or equipment malfunction. These extensions are few and will rarely extend more than a few hours.

State of Nevada
Secretary of State
202 North Carson Street
Carson City, Nevada 89701-4201

Phone: (775) 684 5708

Profit Corporation Fee Schedule
Effective 8-1-01
(Continued)

OTHER PROFIT CORPORATION FEES:

Reinstatement Fee	$200.00
Certificate of Amendment, minimum fee*	$150.00
Certificate pursuant to NRS 78.209 (stock split), minimum fee*	$150.00
Certificate pursuant to NRS 78.1955 (stock designation)	$150.00
Amendment to Certificate pursuant NRS 78.1955 (stock designation)	$150.00
Restated Articles, minimum fee*	$150.00
Certificate of Correction, minimum fee*	$150.00
Certificate of Termination (includes filings pursuant to NRS 78.209, 78.380 and 78.390)	$150.00
Termination of Merger, Exchange or Conversion (filings pursuant to NRS 92A.240)	$325.00
Articles of Merger* or Exchange	$325.00
Dissolution of Corporation	$60.00
Withdrawal of Foreign Corporation	$60.00
Preclearance of any Document	$100.00
Articles of Conversion – contact office for fee information	
Articles of Domestication – contact office for fee information	
Revival of Corporation – contact office for fee information	
24 Hour Expedite fee for above filings	**$100.00**
Change of Resident Agent/Address	$30.00
Resignation of Resident Agent	$40.00
Name Reservation	$20.00
24 Hour Expedite fee for above filings	**$20.00**
Apostille	$20.00
Certificate of Good Standing	$40.00
Initial List of Officers and Directors	$165.00
Annual or Amended List of Officers and Directors	$85.00
24 Hour Expedite fee for above filings	**$50.00**
Certification of Documents – per certification	$20.00
Copies – per page	$1.00
Late Fee for List of Officers	$50.00

*Fee will be higher if stock is increased a significant amount, according to the initial filing fee schedule on page 1 of Profit corporation fee schedule.

2 Hour Expedite is available on all of the above filings at the fee of $500.00 per item.

PLEASE NOTE: the expedite fee is in addition to the standard filing fee charged on each filing and/or order.

24 HOUR EXPEDITE TIME CONSTRAINTS:

Each filing submitted receives same day filing date and may be picked up within 24 hours. Filings to be mailed out no later than the next business day following receipt.

Expedite period begins when filing or service request is received in this office in fileable form.

The Secretary of State reserves the right to extend the expedite period in times of extreme volume, staff shortages, or equipment malfunction. These extensions are few and will rarely extend more than a few hours.

DEAN HELLER
Secretary of State

202 North Carson Street
Carson City, Nevada 89701-4201
Phone: (775) 684 5708

COPIES AND CERTIFICATION SERVICES FEE SCHEDULE

The following is a list of copies and certification services and the associated fees. Fees are per document unless otherwise noted.

SERVICE REQUESTED:

Copies..	$1.00 per page
Certification of Document	$20.00
Search	$40.00
Certificates:	
Certificate of Existence (evidence of good standing ñ short form).................	$40.00
Certificate of Existence (listing amendments ñ long form).............................	$40.00
Certificate Evidencing Name Change	$40.00
Certificate of Fact of Merger..	$40.00
Certificate of Default..	$40.00
Certificate of Revocation	$40.00
Certificate of Dissolution...	$40.00
Certificate of Withdrawal..	$40.00
Certificate of Cancellation..	$40.00
Certificate of Non-Existence..	$40.00
Miscellaneous Certificates..	$40.00
Apostille (Hague Treaty Nations)/Certification (Non-Hague Treaty Nations)	$20.00
Exemplification	$40.00

EXPEDITE SERVICE:

Expedite service is available for copies, certificate and certification services. Fees for expedite service are in addition to the fees as listed above.

24 Hour Expedite Service: Order may be picked up or mailed out within 24-hours.

Copies:	
1 to 10 pages..	$50.00
11 or more pages...	$100.00
Certificates (per entity name):	
1 to 10 certificates...	$50.00
11 or more certificates	$100.00
Search:	
Expedite fee on search only; additional expedite fee required for copies........	$20.00

4-Hour Expedite Service: Order may be picked up and mailed within 4-hours.

CERTIFICATES ONLY (per entity name):	
1 or more certificates	$100.00

BASIC INSTRUCTIONS:

1. All orders may be received in writing with fees enclosed at the above address. Telephone orders with payment by VISA or Mastercard may be called into our Customer Service Department at (775) 684-5708. Trust account and credit card customers may fax *expedite orders only* to (775) 684-5645. Trust account orders must be received on company letterhead.

2. Other than orders specified as a pick-up, all orders are mailed out via first-class mail, unless a prepaid envelope, express mail number or Federal Express number is provided.

3. We *do not* fax orders back to customers. Each order will be returned to one address only.

Nevada Secretary of State Form COPIES1999.01
Revised on: 07/21/01

State of Nevada
Secretary of State
202 North Carson Street
Carson City, Nevada 89701-4201

Phone: (775) 684 5708

SPECIAL SERVICES
SPECIAL SERVICES
24-HOUR
EXPEDITE SERVICE

IMPORTANT: To ensure expedited service, please mark "Expedite" in a conspicuous place at top of the service request. Please indicate method of delivery.

EXPEDITE SERVICE:

The Secretary of State offers a 24-hour expedite service on most filings processed by this office. If you choose to utilize the 24-hour expedite service, please enclose with your filing an additional $100.00 per filing and/or order. Please note that this expedite fee is in addition to the standard filing fee charged on each filing and/or order.

EXPEDITE FEES:

The expedite fee for most services provided by the Secretary of State of State is $100.00 per filing. There are, however, several services that have different expedite fees. The main filings and the associated expedite fees are as follows:

Articles of Incorporation	$100.00
Articles of Organization, Limited Liability Companies	$100.00
Articles of Organization, Limited Liability Partnerships	$100.00
Certificate of Limited Partnership	$100.00
Foreign Qualifications	$100.00
Amendments and Mergers	$100.00
Reinstatement	$100.00
Revivals	$100.00
Preclearance of any document	$100.00
Apostilles	$50.00
Certificate of Good Standing	$50.00
Annual Lists and Late Lists	$50.00
Name Reservation	$20.00
Resident Agent Changes	$20.00
Resident Agent Resignation	$20.00

For information regarding the expedite fee for services not listed above, please call this office at (775) 684-5708.

TIME CONSTRAINTS:

Each filing submitted receives same day filing date and may be picked up within 24 hours. Filings to be mailed will be mailed out no later than the next business day following receipt.

Expedite period begins when filing or service request is received in this office in fileable form.

The Secretary of State reserves the right to extend the expedite period in times of extreme volume, staff shortages, or equipment malfunction. These extensions are few and will rarely extend more than a few hours.

State of Nevada
Secretary of State
202 North Carson Street
Carson City, Nevada 89701-4201

Phone: (775) 684 5708

SPECIAL SERVICES
2-HOUR
EXPEDITE SERVICE

IMPORTANT: To ensure expedited service, please mark "Expedite" in a conspicuous place at top of the service request. Please indicate method of delivery.

2-HOUR EXPEDITE SERVICE:

The Secretary of State offers a 2-hour expedite service on most filings processed by this office. If you choose to utilize the 2-hour expedite service, please enclose with your filing an additional $500.00 per filing and/or order. Please note that this expedite fee is in addition to the standard filing fee charged on each filing and/or order.

IMPORTANT: To ensure 2-hour service, please use 2-hour Expedite Request Form provided by the Secretary of State. Please indicate method of delivery.

For information regarding the 2-hour expedite service, please call this office at (775)684-5708.

TIME CONSTRAINTS:

Each filing submitted for 2-hour expedite receives same day filing date and will be acknowledged by fax or e-mail within 2-hours.* Filings may be picked up within 2-hours. Filings to be mailed will be mailed out no later than the next business day following receipt.
Expedite period begins when filing or service request is received in this office in fileable form.

*Failure to indicate method of acknowledgement (fax or e-mail) or to provide a correct fax number or e-mail address may prevent the Secretary of State from acknowledging the filing of such documents. **For information regarding the expedite fee for services not listed above, please call this office at (775) 684-5708.**

Expedite period begins when filing or service request is received in this office in fileable form.

The Secretary of State reserves the right to extend the expedite period in times of extreme volume, staff shortages, or equipment malfunction. These extensions are few and will rarely extend more than a few minutes.

DEAN HELLER
Secretary of State

SOS Annex
202 North Carson Street
Carson City, Nevada 89701-4201
(775) 684 5708

Credit Card Checklist
(For Counter, Telephone, Fax and Mail Requests)

Service Type: Counter ☐   Telephone ☐   Mail ☐   Fax ☐

Expedite Service: (Requires additional fees) **PLEASE EXPEDITE 24-HOUR SERVICE** ☐   **2-HOUR SERVICE** ☐

Card Type: (the Secretary of State accepts only VISA or MasterCard)

        VISA ☐ or **MasterCard** ☐   **Debit Card** ☐ or **Credit Card** ☐

Customer Credit Card Number: (Must be 16 digits)

| | | | | | | | | | | | | | | | | **V CODE** | | | |

(LAST 3 DIGITS ON BACK OF CREDIT CARD)

Expiration Date:

        Month_____   Year_____

Amount:

        $ _____ _____ . _____ _____ _____ . _____ _____

Cardholder Information:

        Entity Name _____

        Name _____

        Billing Address _____

        City, State, Zip _____

        Telephone _____

Reference Number: (supplied by machine) _____

Approval Number: (supplied by machine) _____

Employee Initials: _____

AUTHORIZATION: CUSTOMER AUTHORIZES THE SECRETARY OF STATE TO BILL AN AMOUNT NOT TO
EXCEED $_____ TO BE CHARGED TO THE ABOVE CREDIT CARD
NUMBER.

_____
(Cardholder signature)

Form **SS-4**
(Rev. December 2001)
Department of the Treasury
Internal Revenue Service

Application for Employer Identification Number
(For use by employers, corporations, partnerships, trusts, estates, churches, government agencies, Indian tribal entities, certain individuals, and others.)
▶ See separate instructions for each line. ▶ Keep a copy for your records.

EIN

OMB No. 1545-0003

Type or print clearly.

1 Legal name of entity (or individual) for whom the EIN is being requested

2 Trade name of business (if different from name on line 1)

3 Executor, trustee, "care of" name

4a Mailing address (room, apt., suite no. and street, or P.O. box)

5a Street address (if different) (Do not enter a P.O. box.)

4b City, state, and ZIP code

5b City, state, and ZIP code

6 County and state where principal business is located

7a Name of principal officer, general partner, grantor, owner, or trustor

7b SSN, ITIN, or EIN

8a Type of entity (check only one box)
☐ Sole proprietor (SSN) _____
☐ Partnership
☐ Corporation (enter form number to be filed) ▶ _____
☐ Personal service corp.
☐ Church or church-controlled organization
☐ Other nonprofit organization (specify) ▶ _____
☐ Other (specify) ▶

☐ Estate (SSN of decedent) _____
☐ Plan administrator (SSN) _____
☐ Trust (SSN of grantor) _____
☐ National Guard ☐ State/local government
☐ Farmers' cooperative ☐ Federal government/military
☐ REMIC ☐ Indian tribal governments/enterprises
Group Exemption Number (GEN) ▶ _____

8b If a corporation, name the state or foreign country (if applicable) where incorporated

State

Foreign country

9 Reason for applying (check only one box)
☐ Started new business (specify type) ▶ _____
☐ Hired employees (Check the box and see line 12.)
☐ Compliance with IRS withholding regulations
☐ Other (specify) ▶

☐ Banking purpose (specify purpose) ▶ _____
☐ Changed type of organization (specify new type) ▶ _____
☐ Purchased going business
☐ Created a trust (specify type) ▶ _____
☐ Created a pension plan (specify type) ▶ _____

10 Date business started or acquired (month, day, year)

11 Closing month of accounting year

12 First date wages or annuities were paid or will be paid (month, day, year). **Note:** If applicant is a withholding agent, enter date income will first be paid to nonresident alien. (month, day, year) . . . . ▶

13 Highest number of employees expected in the next 12 months. **Note:** If the applicant does not expect to have any employees during the period, enter "-0-." . . . . ▶

Agricultural	Household	Other

14 Check **one** box that best describes the principal activity of your business.
☐ Construction ☐ Rental & leasing ☐ Transportation & warehousing ☐ Health care & social assistance ☐ Wholesale-agent/broker
☐ Real estate ☐ Manufacturing ☐ Finance & insurance ☐ Accommodation & food service ☐ Wholesale-other ☐ Retail
☐ Other (specify)

15 Indicate principal line of merchandise sold; specific construction work done; products produced; or services provided.

16a Has the applicant ever applied for an employer identification number for this or any other business? . . . . . ☐ Yes ☐ No
Note: If "Yes," please complete lines 16b and 16c.

16b If you checked "Yes" on line 16a, give applicant's legal name and trade name shown on prior application if different from line 1 or 2 above.
Legal name ▶   Trade name ▶

16c Approximate date when, and city and state where, the application was filed. Enter previous employer identification number if known.
Approximate date when filed (mo., day, year) | City and state where filed | Previous EIN

Third Party Designee

Complete this section **only** if you want to authorize the named individual to receive the entity's EIN and answer questions about the completion of this form.

Designee's name

Address and ZIP code

Designee's telephone number (include area code)
( )

Designee's fax number (include area code)
( )

Under penalties of perjury, I declare that I have examined this application, and to the best of my knowledge and belief, it is true, correct, and complete.

Name and title (type or print clearly) ▶

Signature ▶   Date ▶

Applicant's telephone number (include area code)
( )

Applicant's fax number (include area code)
( )

For Privacy Act and Paperwork Reduction Act Notice, see separate instructions.   Cat. No. 16055N   Form **SS-4** (Rev. 12-2001)

Do I Need an EIN?

File Form SS-4 if the applicant entity does not already have an EIN but is required to show an EIN on any return, statement, or other document.[1] **See also the separate instructions for each line on Form SS-4.**

IF the applicant...	AND...	THEN...
Started a new business	Does not currently have (nor expect to have) employees	Complete lines 1, 2, 4a- 6, 8a, and 9- 16c.
Hired (or will hire) employees, including household employees	Does not already have an EIN	Complete lines 1, 2, 4a- 6, 7a- b (if applicable), 8a, 8b (if applicable), and 9- 16c.
Opened a bank account	Needs an EIN for banking purposes only	Complete lines 1- 5b, 7a- b (if applicable), 8a, 9, and 16a- c.
Changed type of organization	Either the legal character of the organization or its ownership changed (e.g., you incorporate a sole proprietorship or form a partnership)[2]	Complete lines 1- 16c (as applicable).
Purchased a going business[3]	Does not already have an EIN	Complete lines 1- 16c (as applicable).
Created a trust	The trust is other than a grantor trust or an IRA trust[4]	Complete lines 1- 16c (as applicable).
Created a pension plan as a plan administrator[5]	Needs an EIN for reporting purposes	Complete lines 1, 2, 4a- 6, 8a, 9, and 16a- c.
Is a foreign person needing an EIN to comply with IRS withholding regulations	Needs an EIN to complete a Form W-8 (other than Form W-8ECI), avoid withholding on portfolio assets, or claim tax treaty benefits[6]	Complete lines 1- 5b, 7a- b (SSN or ITIN optional), 8a- 9, and 16a- c.
Is administering an estate	Needs an EIN to report estate income on Form 1041	Complete lines 1, 3, 4a- b, 8a, 9, and 16a- c.
Is a withholding agent for taxes on non-wage income paid to an alien (i.e., individual, corporation, or partnership, etc.)	Is an agent, broker, fiduciary, manager, tenant, or spouse who is required to file **Form 1042,** Annual Withholding Tax Return for U.S. Source Income of Foreign Persons	Complete lines 1, 2, 3 (if applicable), 4a- 5b, 7a- b (if applicable), 8a, 9, and 16a- c.
Is a state or local agency	Serves as a tax reporting agent for public assistance recipients under Rev. Proc. 80-4, 1980-1 C.B. 581[7]	Complete lines 1, 2, 4a- 5b, 8a, 9, and 16a- c.
Is a single-member LLC	Needs an EIN to file **Form 8832,** Classification Election, for filing employment tax returns, **or** for state reporting purposes[8]	Complete lines 1- 16c (as applicable).
Is an S corporation	Needs an EIN to file **Form 2553,** Election by a Small Business Corporation[9]	Complete lines 1- 16c (as applicable).

[1] For example, a sole proprietorship or self-employed farmer who establishes a qualified retirement plan, or is required to file excise, employment, alcohol, tobacco, or firearms returns, must have an EIN. **A partnership, corporation, REMIC (real estate mortgage investment conduit), nonprofit organization (church, club, etc.), or farmers' cooperative must use an EIN for any tax-related purpose even if the entity does not have employees.**

[2] However, **do not** apply for a new EIN if the existing entity only **(a)** changed its business name, **(b)** elected on Form 8832 to change the way it is taxed (or is covered by the default rules), or **(c)** terminated its partnership status because at least 50% of the total interests in partnership capital and profits were sold or exchanged within a 12-month period. (The EIN of the terminated partnership should continue to be used. See Regulations section 301.6109-1(d)(2)(iii).)

[3] Do not use the EIN of the prior business unless you became the "owner" of a corporation by acquiring its stock.

[4] However, IRA trusts that are required to file **Form 990-T,** Exempt Organization Business Income Tax Return, must have an EIN.

[5] A plan administrator is the person or group of persons specified as the administrator by the instrument under which the plan is operated.

[6] Entities applying to be a Qualified Intermediary (QI) need a QI-EIN even if they already have an EIN. **See Rev. Proc. 2000-12.**

[7] See also *Household employer* on page 4. (**Note:** State or local agencies may need an EIN for other reasons, e.g., hired employees.)

[8] Most LLCs **do not** need to file Form 8832. See **Limited liability company (LLC)** on page 4 for details on completing Form SS-4 for an LLC.

[9] An existing corporation that is electing or revoking S corporation status should use its previously-assigned EIN.

Instructions for Form SS-4

Department of the Treasury
Internal Revenue Service

(Rev. December 2001)

Application for Employer Identification Number

Section references are to the Internal Revenue Code unless otherwise noted.

General Instructions

Use these instructions to complete **Form SS-4,**
Application for Employer Identification Number. Also see
Do I Need an EIN? on page 2 of Form SS-4.

Purpose of Form

Use Form SS-4 to apply for an employer identification
number (EIN). An EIN is a nine-digit number (for
example, 12-3456789) assigned to sole proprietors,
corporations, partnerships, estates, trusts, and other
entities for tax filing and reporting purposes. The
information you provide on this form will establish your
business tax account.

> ⚠ **CAUTION** An EIN is for use in connection with your business
> activities only. Do **not** use your EIN in place of
> your social security number (SSN).

File only one Form SS-4. Generally, a sole proprietor
should file only one Form SS-4 and needs only one EIN,
regardless of the number of businesses operated as a
sole proprietorship or trade names under which a
business operates. However, if the proprietorship
incorporates or enters into a partnership, a new EIN is
required. Also, each corporation in an affiliated group
must have its own EIN.

EIN applied for, but not received. If you do not have an
EIN by the time a **return** is due, write "Applied For" and
the date you applied in the space shown for the number.
Do not show your social security number (SSN) as an
EIN on returns.

If you do not have an EIN by the time a **tax deposit** is
due, send your payment to the Internal Revenue Service
Center for your filing area as shown in the instructions for
the form that you are filing. Make your check or
money order payable to the **"United States Treasury"**
and show your name (as shown on Form SS-4), address,
type of tax, period covered, and date you applied for an
EIN.

Related Forms and Publications

The following **forms** and **instructions** may be useful to
filers of Form SS-4:
- **Form 990-T,** Exempt Organization Business Income
Tax Return
- **Instructions for Form 990-T**
- **Schedule C (Form 1040),** Profit or Loss From
Business
- **Schedule F (Form 1040),** Profit or Loss From Farming
- **Instructions for Form 1041 and Schedules A, B, D,
G, I, J, and K-1,** U.S. Income Tax Return for Estates and
Trusts

- **Form 1042,** Annual Withholding Tax Return for U.S.
Source Income of Foreign Persons
- **Instructions for Form 1065,** U.S. Return of
Partnership Income
- **Instructions for Form 1066,** U.S. Real Estate
Mortgage Investment Conduit (REMIC) Income Tax
Return
- **Instructions for Forms 1120 and 1120-A**
- **Form 2553,** Election by a Small Business Corporation
- **Form 2848,** Power of Attorney and Declaration of
Representative
- **Form 8821,** Tax Information Authorization
- **Form 8832,** Entity Classification Election
For more **information** about filing Form SS-4 and
related issues, see:
- **Circular A,** Agricultural Employer's Tax Guide
(Pub. 51)
- **Circular E,** Employer's Tax Guide (Pub. 15)
- **Pub. 538,** Accounting Periods and Methods
- **Pub. 542,** Corporations
- **Pub. 557,** Exempt Status for Your Organization
- **Pub. 583,** Starting a Business and Keeping Records
- **Pub. 966,** EFTPS: Now a Full Range of Electronic
Choices to Pay All Your Federal Taxes
- **Pub. 1635,** Understanding Your EIN
- **Package 1023,** Application for Recognition of
Exemption
- **Package 1024,** Application for Recognition of
Exemption Under Section 501(a)

How To Get Forms and Publications

Phone. You can order forms, instructions, and
publications by phone 24 hours a day, 7 days a week.
Just call 1-800-TAX-FORM (1-800-829-3676). You
should receive your order or notification of its status
within 10 workdays.

Personal computer. With your personal computer and
modem, you can get the forms and information you need
using the IRS Web Site at **www.irs.gov** or File Transfer
Protocol at **ftp.irs.gov.**

CD-ROM. For small businesses, return preparers, or
others who may frequently need tax forms or
publications, a CD-ROM containing over 2,000 tax
products (including many prior year forms) can be
purchased from the National Technical Information
Service (NTIS).

To order **Pub. 1796,** Federal Tax Products on
CD-ROM, call **1-877-CDFORMS** (1-877-233-6767) toll
free or connect to **www.irs.gov/cdorders.**

Cat. No. 62736F

Tax Help for Your Business

IRS-sponsored Small Business Workshops provide information about your Federal and state tax obligations. For information about workshops in your area, call 1-800-829-1040 and ask for your Taxpayer Education Coordinator.

How To Apply

You can apply for an EIN by telephone, fax, or mail depending on how soon you need to use the EIN.

Application by Tele-TIN. Under the Tele-TIN program, you can receive your EIN by telephone and use it immediately to file a return or make a payment. To receive an EIN by telephone, IRS suggests that you complete Form SS-4 so that you will have all relevant information available. Then call the Tele-TIN number at 1-866-816-2065. (International applicants must call 215-516-6999.) Tele-TIN hours of operation are 7:30 a.m. to 5:30 p.m. The person making the call must be authorized to sign the form or be an authorized designee. See **Signature** and **Third Party Designee** on page 6. Also see the **TIP** below.

An IRS representative will use the information from the Form SS-4 to establish your account and assign you an EIN. Write the number you are given on the upper right corner of the form and sign and date it. Keep this copy for your records.

If requested by an IRS representative, mail or fax (facsimile) the signed Form SS-4 (including any Third Party Designee authorization) **within 24 hours** to the Tele-TIN Unit at the service center address provided by the IRS representative.

TIP *Taxpayer representatives can use Tele-TIN to apply for an EIN on behalf of their client and request that the EIN be faxed to their **client** on the same day. (**Note:** By utilizing this procedure, you are authorizing the IRS to fax the EIN without a cover sheet.)*

Application by Fax-TIN. Under the Fax-TIN program, you can receive your EIN by fax within 4 business days. Complete and fax Form SS-4 to the IRS using the Fax-TIN number listed below for your state. A long-distance charge to callers outside of the local calling area will apply. Fax-TIN numbers can only be used to apply for an EIN. **The numbers may change without notice.** Fax-TIN is available 24 hours a day, 7 days a week.

Be sure to provide your fax number so that IRS can fax Form SS-4 back to you. (**Note:** By utilizing this procedure, you are authorizing the IRS to fax the EIN without a cover sheet.)

Do not call Tele-TIN for the same entity because duplicate EINs may be issued. See **Third Party Designee** on page 6.

Application by mail. Complete Form SS-4 at least 4 to 5 weeks before you will need an EIN. Sign and date the application and mail it to the service center address for your state. You will receive your EIN in the mail in approximately 4 weeks. See also **Third Party Designee** on page 6.

Call 1-800-829-1040 to verify a number or to ask about the status of an application by mail.

If your principal business, office or agency, or legal residence in the case of an individual, is located In:	Call the Tele-TIN or Fax-TIN number shown or file with the "Internal Revenue Service Center" at:
Connecticut, Delaware, District of Columbia, Florida, Georgia, Maine, Maryland, Massachusetts, New Hampshire, New Jersey, New York, North Carolina, Ohio, Pennsylvania, Rhode Island, South Carolina, Vermont, Virginia, West Virginia	Attn: EIN Operation Holtsville, NY 00501 Tele-TIN 866-816-2065 Fax-TIN 631-447-8960
Illinois, Indiana, Kentucky, Michigan	Attn: EIN Operation Cincinnati, OH 45999 Tele-TIN 866-816-2065 Fax-TIN 859-669-5760
Alabama, Alaska, Arizona, Arkansas, California, Colorado, Hawaii, Idaho, Iowa, Kansas, Louisiana, Minnesota, Mississippi, Missouri, Montana, Nebraska, Nevada, New Mexico, North Dakota, Oklahoma, Oregon, Puerto Rico, South Dakota, Tennessee, Texas, Utah, Washington, Wisconsin, Wyoming	Attn: EIN Operation Philadelphia, PA 19255 Tele-TIN 866-816-2065 Fax-TIN 215-516-3990
If you have no legal residence, principal place of business, or principal office or agency in any state:	Attn: EIN Operation Philadelphia, PA 19255 Tele-TIN 215-516-6999 Fax-TIN 215-516-3990

Specific Instructions

Print or type all entries on Form SS-4. Follow the instructions for each line to expedite processing and to avoid unnecessary IRS requests for additional information. Enter "N/A" (nonapplicable) on the lines that do not apply.

Line 1—Legal name of entity (or individual) for whom the EIN is being requested. Enter the legal name of the entity (or individual) applying for the EIN exactly as it appears on the social security card, charter, or other applicable legal document.

Individuals. Enter your first name, middle initial, and last name. If you are a sole proprietor, enter your individual name, not your business name. Enter your business name on line 2. Do not use abbreviations or nicknames on line 1.

Trusts. Enter the name of the trust.

Estate of a decedent. Enter the name of the estate.

Partnerships. Enter the legal name of the partnership as it appears in the partnership agreement.

Corporations. Enter the corporate name as it appears in the corporation charter or other legal document creating it.

Plan administrators. Enter the name of the plan administrator. A plan administrator who already has an EIN should use that number.

Line 2—Trade name of business. Enter the trade name of the business if different from the legal name. The trade name is the "doing business as " (DBA) name.

 *Use the full legal name shown on line 1 on all tax returns filed for the entity. (However, if you enter a trade name on line 2 and choose to use the trade name instead of the legal name, enter the trade name on **all returns** you file.) To prevent processing delays and errors, **always** use the legal name only (or the trade name only) on **all** tax returns.*

Line 3—Executor, trustee, "care of" name. Trusts enter the name of the trustee. Estates enter the name of the executor, administrator, or other fiduciary. If the entity applying has a designated person to receive tax information, enter that person's name as the "care of" person. Enter the individual's first name, middle initial, and last name.

Lines 4a-b—Mailing address. Enter the mailing address for the entity's correspondence. If line 3 is completed, enter the address for the executor, trustee or "care of" person. Generally, this address will be used on all tax returns.

TIP *File **Form 8822**, Change of Address, to report any subsequent changes to the entity's mailing address.*

Lines 5a-b—Street address. Provide the entity's physical address **only** if different from its mailing address shown in lines 4a-b. **Do not** enter a P.O. box number here.

Line 6—County and state where principal business is located. Enter the entity's primary **physical** location.

Lines 7a-b—Name of principal officer, general partner, grantor, owner, or trustor. Enter the first name, middle initial, last name, and SSN of **(a)** the principal officer if the business is a corporation, **(b)** a general partner if a partnership, **(c)** the owner of an entity that is disregarded as separate from its owner (disregarded entities owned by a corporation enter the corporation's name and EIN), or **(d)** a grantor, owner, or trustor if a trust.

If the person in question is an **alien individual** with a previously assigned individual taxpayer identification number (ITIN), enter the ITIN in the space provided and submit a copy of an official identifying document. If necessary, complete **Form W-7**, Application for IRS Individual Taxpayer Identification Number, to obtain an ITIN.

You are **required** to enter an SSN, ITIN, or EIN unless the only reason you are applying for an EIN is to make an entity classification election (see Regulations section 301.7701-1 through 301.7701-3) and you are a nonresident alien with no effectively connected income from sources within the United States.

Line 8a—Type of entity. Check the box that best describes the type of entity applying for the EIN. If you are an alien individual with an ITIN previously assigned to you, enter the ITIN in place of a requested SSN.

 *This is not an election for a tax classification of an entity. See **"Limited liability company (LLC)"** on page 4.*

Other. If not specifically mentioned, check the "Other" box, enter the type of entity and the type of return, if any, that will be filed (for example, "Common Trust Fund, Form 1065" or "Created a Pension Plan"). Do not enter "N/A." If you are an alien individual applying for an EIN, see the **Lines 7a-b** instructions above.
- **Household employer.** If you are an individual, check the "Other" box and enter "Household Employer" and your SSN. If you are a state or local agency serving as a tax reporting agent for public assistance recipients who become household employers, check the "Other" box and enter "Household Employer Agent." If you are a trust that qualifies as a household employer, you do not need a separate EIN for reporting tax information relating to household employees; use the EIN of the trust.
- **QSub.** For a qualified subchapter S subsidiary (QSub) check the "Other" box and specify "QSub."
- **Withholding agent.** If you are a withholding agent required to file Form 1042, check the "Other" box and enter "Withholding Agent."

Sole proprietor. Check this box if you file Schedule C, C-EZ, or F (Form 1040) and have a qualified plan, or are required to file excise, employment, or alcohol, tobacco, or firearms returns, or are a payer of gambling winnings. Enter your SSN (or ITIN) in the space provided. If you are a nonresident alien with no effectively connected income from sources within the United States, you do not need to enter an SSN or ITIN.

Corporation. This box is for any corporation **other than a personal service corporation.** If you check this box, enter the income tax form number to be filed by the entity in the space provided.

 *If you entered "1120S" after the "Corporation" checkbox, the corporation **must** file Form 2553 no later than the 15th day of the 3rd month of the tax year the election is to take effect. Until Form 2553 has been received and approved, you will be considered a Form 1120 filer. See the Instructions for Form 2553.*

Personal service corp. Check this box if the entity is a personal service corporation. An entity is a personal service corporation for a tax year only if:
- The principal activity of the entity during the testing period (prior tax year) for the tax year is the performance of personal services substantially by employee-owners, and
- The employee-owners own at least 10% of the fair market value of the outstanding stock in the entity on the last day of the testing period.

Personal services include performance of services in such fields as health, law, accounting, or consulting. For more information about personal service corporations, see the Instructions for Forms 1120 and 1120-A and Pub. 542.

    Other nonprofit organization. Check this box if the nonprofit organization is other than a church or church-controlled organization and specify the type of nonprofit organization (for example, an educational organization).

 *If the organization also seeks tax-exempt status, you **must** file either Package 1023 or Package 1024. See Pub. 557 for more information.*

    If the organization is covered by a group exemption letter, enter the four-digit **group exemption number (GEN).** (Do not confuse the GEN with the nine-digit EIN.) If you do not know the GEN, contact the parent organization. Get Pub. 557 for more information about group exemption numbers.

    Plan administrator. If the plan administrator is an individual, enter the plan administrator's SSN in the space provided.

    REMIC. Check this box if the entity has elected to be treated as a real estate mortgage investment conduit (REMIC). See the Instructions for Form 1066 for more information.

Limited liability company (LLC). An LLC is an entity organized under the laws of a state or foreign country as a limited liability company. For Federal tax purposes, an LLC may be treated as a partnership or corporation or be disregarded as an entity separate from its owner.

    By **default,** a domestic LLC with only one member is **disregarded** as an entity separate from its owner and must include all of its income and expenses on the owner's tax return (e.g., **Schedule C (Form 1040)**). Also by default, a domestic LLC with two or more members is treated as a partnership. A domestic LLC may file Form 8832 to avoid either default classification and elect to be classified as an association taxable as a corporation. For more information on entity classifications (including the rules for foreign entities), see the instructions for Form 8832.

 *Do not file Form 8832 if the LLC accepts the default classifications above. **However, if the LLC will be electing S Corporation status, it must timely file both Form 8832 and Form 2553.***

    Complete Form SS-4 for LLCs as follows:
● A single-member, domestic LLC that accepts the default classification (above) does not need an EIN and generally should not file Form SS-4. Generally, the LLC should use the name and EIN of its **owner** for all Federal tax purposes. However, the reporting and payment of employment taxes for employees of the LLC may be made using the name and EIN of **either** the owner or the LLC as explained in Notice 99-6, 1999-1 C.B. 321. You can find Notice 99-6 on page 12 of Internal Revenue Bulletin 1999-3 at **www.irs.gov. (Note:** If the LLC-applicant indicates in box 13 that it has employees or expects to have employees, the owner (whether an individual or other entity) of a single-member domestic LLC will also be assigned its own EIN (if it does not

already have one) even if the LLC will be filing the employment tax returns.)
● A single-member, domestic LLC that accepts the default classification (above) and wants an EIN for filing employment tax returns (see above) or non-Federal purposes, such as a state requirement, must check the "Other" box and write "Disregarded Entity" or, when applicable, "Disregarded Entity—Sole Proprietorship" in the space provided.
● A multi-member, domestic LLC that accepts the default classification (above) must check the "Partnership" box.
● A domestic LLC that will be filing Form 8832 to elect corporate status must check the "Corporation" box and write in "Single-Member" or "Multi-Member" immediately below the "form number" entry line.

Line 9—Reason for applying. Check only **one** box. Do not enter "N/A."

    Started new business. Check this box if you are starting a new business that requires an EIN. If you check this box, enter the type of business being started. **Do not** apply if you already have an EIN and are only adding another place of business.

    Hired employees. Check this box if the existing business is requesting an EIN because it has hired or is hiring employees and is therefore required to file employment tax returns. **Do not** apply if you already have an EIN and are only hiring employees. For information on employment taxes (e.g., for family members), see Circular E.

 You may be required to make electronic deposits of all depository taxes (such as employment tax, excise tax, and corporate income tax) using the Electronic Federal Tax Payment System (EFTPS). See section 11, Depositing Taxes, of Circular E and Pub. 966.

    Created a pension plan. Check this box if you have created a pension plan and need an EIN for reporting purposes. Also, enter the type of plan in the space provided.

 Check this box if you are applying for a trust EIN when a new pension plan is established. In addition, check the "Other" box in line 8a and write "Created a Pension Plan" in the space provided.

    Banking purpose. Check this box if you are requesting an EIN for banking purposes only, and enter the banking purpose (for example, a bowling league for depositing dues or an investment club for dividend and interest reporting).

    Changed type of organization. Check this box if the business is changing its type of organization. For example, the business was a sole proprietorship and has been incorporated or has become a partnership. If you check this box, specify in the space provided (including available space immediately below) the type of change made. For example, "From Sole Proprietorship to Partnership."

    Purchased going business. Check this box if you purchased an existing business. **Do not** use the former owner's EIN unless you became the "owner" of a corporation by acquiring its stock.

Created a trust. Check this box if you created a trust, and enter the type of trust created. For example, indicate if the trust is a nonexempt charitable trust or a split-interest trust.

Exception. Do **not** file this form for certain grantor-type trusts. The trustee does not need an EIN for the trust if the trustee furnishes the name and TIN of the grantor/owner and the address of the trust to all payors. See the Instructions for Form 1041 for more information.

 Do not *check this box if you are applying for a trust EIN when a new pension plan is established. Check "Created a pension plan."*

Other. Check this box if you are requesting an EIN for any other reason; and enter the reason. For example, a newly-formed state government entity should enter "Newly-Formed State Government Entity" in the space provided.

Line 10—Date business started or acquired. If you are starting a new business, enter the starting date of the business. If the business you acquired is already operating, enter the date you acquired the business. Trusts should enter the date the trust was legally created. Estates should enter the date of death of the decedent whose name appears on line 1 or the date when the estate was legally funded.

Line 11—Closing month of accounting year. Enter the last month of your accounting year or tax year. An accounting or tax year is usually 12 consecutive months, either a calendar year or a fiscal year (including a period of 52 or 53 weeks). A calendar year is 12 consecutive months ending on December 31. A fiscal year is either 12 consecutive months ending on the last day of any month other than December or a 52-53 week year. For more information on accounting periods, see Pub. 538.

Individuals. Your tax year generally will be a calendar year.

Partnerships. Partnerships must adopt one of the following tax years:
• The tax year of the majority of its partners,
• The tax year common to all of its principal partners,
• The tax year that results in the least aggregate deferral of income, or
• In certain cases, some other tax year.
    See the Instructions for Form 1065 for more information.

REMICs. REMICs must have a calendar year as their tax year.

Personal service corporations. A personal service corporation generally must adopt a calendar year unless:
• It can establish a business purpose for having a different tax year, or
• It elects under section 444 to have a tax year other than a calendar year.

Trusts. Generally, a trust must adopt a calendar year except for the following:
• Tax-exempt trusts,
• Charitable trusts, and
• Grantor-owned trusts.

Line 12—First date wages or annuities were paid or will be paid. If the business has or will have employees, enter the date on which the business began or will begin to pay wages. If the business does not plan to have employees, enter "N/A."

Withholding agent. Enter the date you began or will begin to pay income (including annuities) to a nonresident alien. This also applies to individuals who are required to file Form 1042 to report alimony paid to a nonresident alien.

Line 13—Highest number of employees expected in the next 12 months. Complete each box by entering the number (including zero ("-0-")) of "Agricultural," "Household," or "Other" employees expected by the applicant in the next 12 months. For a definition of agricultural labor (farmwork), see Circular A.

Lines 14 and 15. Check the **one** box in line 14 that best describes the principal activity of the applicant's business. Check the "Other" box (and specify the applicant's principal activity) if none of the listed boxes applies.

Use line 15 to describe the applicant's principal line of business in more detail. For example, if you checked the "Construction" box in line 14, enter additional detail such as "General contractor for residential buildings" in line 15.

 Do not complete lines 14 and 15 if you entered zero "(-0-)" in line 13.

Construction. Check this box if the applicant is engaged in erecting buildings or other structures, (e.g., streets, highways, bridges, tunnels). The term "Construction" also includes special trade contractors, (e.g., plumbing, HVAC, electrical, carpentry, concrete, excavation, etc. contractors).

Real estate. Check this box if the applicant is engaged in renting or leasing real estate to others; managing, selling, buying or renting real estate for others; or providing related real estate services (e.g., appraisal services).

Rental and leasing. Check this box if the applicant is engaged in providing tangible goods such as autos, computers, consumer goods, or industrial machinery and equipment to customers in return for a periodic rental or lease payment.

Manufacturing. Check this box if the applicant is engaged in the mechanical, physical, or chemical transformation of materials, substances, or components into new products. The assembling of component parts of manufactured products is also considered to be manufacturing.

Transportation & warehousing. Check this box if the applicant provides transportation of passengers or cargo; warehousing or storage of goods; scenic or sight-seeing transportation; or support activities related to these modes of transportation.

Finance & insurance. Check this box if the applicant is engaged in transactions involving the creation, liquidation, or change of ownership of financial assets and/or facilitating such financial transactions;

underwriting annuities/insurance policies; facilitating such underwriting by selling insurance policies; or by providing other insurance or employee-benefit related services.

Health care and social assistance. Check this box if the applicant is engaged in providing physical, medical, or psychiatric care using licensed health care professionals or providing social assistance activities such as youth centers, adoption agencies, individual/family services, temporary shelters, etc.

Accommodation & food services. Check this box if the applicant is engaged in providing customers with lodging, meal preparation, snacks, or beverages for immediate consumption.

Wholesale–agent/broker. Check this box if the applicant is engaged in arranging for the purchase or sale of goods owned by others or purchasing goods on a commission basis for goods traded in the wholesale market, usually between businesses.

Wholesale–other. Check this box if the applicant is engaged in selling goods in the wholesale market generally to other businesses for resale on their own account.

Retail. Check this box if the applicant is engaged in selling merchandise to the general public from a fixed store; by direct, mail-order, or electronic sales; or by using vending machines.

Other. Check this box if the applicant is engaged in an activity not described above. Describe the applicant's principal business activity in the space provided.

Lines 16a-c. Check the applicable box in line 16a to indicate whether or not the entity (or individual) applying for an EIN was issued one previously. Complete lines 16b and 16c **only** if the "Yes" box in line 16a is checked. If the applicant previously applied for **more than one** EIN, write "See Attached" in the empty space in line 16a and attach a separate sheet providing the line 16b and 16c information for each EIN previously requested.

Third Party Designee. Complete this section **only** if you want to authorize the named individual to receive the entity's EIN and answer questions about the completion of Form SS-4. The designee's authority terminates at the time the EIN is assigned and released to the designee. **You must complete the signature area for the authorization to be valid.**

Signature. When required, the application must be signed by **(a)** the individual, if the applicant is an individual, **(b)** the president, vice president, or other principal officer, if the applicant is a corporation, **(c)** a responsible and duly authorized member or officer having knowledge of its affairs, if the applicant is a partnership, government entity, or other unincorporated organization, or **(d)** the fiduciary, if the applicant is a trust or an estate. Foreign applicants may have any duly-authorized person, (e.g., division manager), sign Form SS-4.

Privacy Act and Paperwork Reduction Act Notice. We ask for the information on this form to carry out the Internal Revenue laws of the United States. We need it to comply with section 6109 and the regulations thereunder which generally require the inclusion of an employer identification number (EIN) on certain returns, statements, or other documents filed with the Internal Revenue Service. If your entity is required to obtain an EIN, you are required to provide all of the information requested on this form. Information on this form may be used to determine which Federal tax returns you are required to file and to provide you with related forms and publications.

We disclose this form to the Social Security Administration for their use in determining compliance with applicable laws. We may give this information to the Department of Justice for use in civil and criminal litigation, and to the cities, states, and the District of Columbia for use in administering their tax laws. We may also disclose this information to Federal, state, or local agencies that investigate or respond to acts or threats of terrorism or participate in intelligence or counterintelligence activities concerning terrorism.

We will be unable to issue an EIN to you unless you provide all of the requested information which applies to your entity. Providing false information could subject you to penalties.

You are not required to provide the information requested on a form that is subject to the Paperwork Reduction Act unless the form displays a valid OMB control number. Books or records relating to a form or its instructions must be retained as long as their contents may become material in the administration of any Internal Revenue law. Generally, tax returns and return information are confidential, as required by section 6103.

The time needed to complete and file this form will vary depending on individual circumstances. The estimated average time is:

Recordkeeping	6 min.
Learning about the law or the form	22 min.
Preparing the form	46 min.
Copying, assembling, and sending the form to the IRS	20 min.

If you have comments concerning the accuracy of these time estimates or suggestions for making this form simpler, we would be happy to hear from you. You can write to the Tax Forms Committee, Western Area Distribution Center, Rancho Cordova, CA 95743-0001. **Do not** send the form to this address. Instead, see **How To Apply** on page 2.

Form **2553** (Rev. December 2002) Department of the Treasury Internal Revenue Service	**Election by a Small Business Corporation** (Under section 1362 of the Internal Revenue Code) ▶ See Parts II and III on back and the separate instructions. ▶ The corporation may either send or fax this form to the IRS. See page 2 of the instructions.	OMB No. 1545-0146

Notes:
1. *Do not file* **Form 1120S**, *U.S. Income Tax Return for an S Corporation, for any tax year before the year the election takes effect.*
2. *This election to be an S corporation can be accepted only if all the tests are met under* **Who May Elect** *on page 1 of the instructions; all shareholders have signed the consent statement; and the exact name and address of the corporation and other required form information are provided.*
3. *If the corporation was in existence before the effective date of this election, see* **Taxes an S Corporation May Owe** *on page 1 of the instructions.*

Part I	**Election Information**		

Please Type or Print

Name of corporation (see instructions)	**A** Employer identification number
Number, street, and room or suite no. (If a P.O. box, see instructions.)	**B** Date incorporated
City or town, state, and ZIP code	**C** State of incorporation

D Check the applicable box(es) if the corporation, after applying for the EIN shown in **A** above, changed its name ☐ or address ☐

E Election is to be effective for tax year beginning (month, day, year) . . . . ▶   /   /

F Name and title of officer or legal representative who the IRS may call for more information

G Telephone number of officer or legal representative
(   )

H If this election takes effect for the first tax year the corporation exists, enter month, day, and year of the **earliest** of the following: (1) date the corporation first had shareholders, (2) date the corporation first had assets, or (3) date the corporation began doing business . . . . ▶   /   /

I Selected tax year: Annual return will be filed for tax year ending (month and day) ▶- -
If the tax year ends on any date other than December 31, except for a 52–53-week tax year ending with reference to the month of December, you **must** complete Part II on the back. If the date you enter is the ending date of a 52–53-week tax year, write "52–53-week year" to the right of the date.

J Name and address of each shareholder; shareholder's spouse having a community property interest in the corporation's stock; and each tenant in common, joint tenant, and tenant by the entirety. (A husband and wife (and their estates) are counted as one shareholder in determining the number of shareholders without regard to the manner in which the stock is owned.)	**K** Shareholders' Consent Statement. Under penalties of perjury, we declare that we consent to the election of the above-named corporation to be an S corporation under section 1362(a) and that we have examined this consent statement, including accompanying schedules and statements, and to the best of our knowledge and belief, it is true, correct, and complete. We understand our consent is binding and may not be withdrawn after the corporation has made a valid election. (Shareholders sign and date below.)		**L** Stock owned		**M** Social security number or employer identification number (see instructions)	**N** Share-holder's tax year ends (month and day)
	Signature	Date	Number of shares	Dates acquired		

Under penalties of perjury, I declare that I have examined this election, including accompanying schedules and statements, and to the best of my knowledge and belief, it is true, correct, and complete.

Signature of officer ▶   Title ▶   Date ▶

For Paperwork Reduction Act Notice, see page 4 of the instructions.   Cat. No. 18629R   Form **2553** (Rev. 12-2002)

Form 2553 (Rev. 12-2002)   Page **2**

Part II   Selection of Fiscal Tax Year (All corporations using this part must complete item O and item P, Q, or R.)

O   Check the applicable box to indicate whether the corporation is:

    1. ☐ A new corporation adopting the tax year entered in item I, Part I.

    2. ☐ An existing corporation retaining the tax year entered in item I, Part I.

    3. ☐ An existing corporation changing to the tax year entered in item I, Part I.

P   Complete item P if the corporation is using the automatic approval provisions of Rev. Proc. 2002-38, 2002-22 I.R.B. 1037, to request **(1)** a natural business year (as defined in section 5.05 of Rev. Proc. 2002-38) or **(2)** a year that satisfies the ownership tax year test (as defined in section 5.06 of Rev. Proc. 2002-38). Check the applicable box below to indicate the representation statement the corporation is making.

    1. Natural Business Year ▶ ☐ I represent that the corporation is adopting, retaining, or changing to a tax year that qualifies as its natural business year as defined in section 5.05 of Rev. Proc. 2002-38 and has attached a statement verifying that it satisfies the 25% gross receipts test (see instructions for content of statement). I also represent that the corporation is not precluded by section 4.02 of Rev. Proc. 2002-38 from obtaining automatic approval of such adoption, retains, or change in tax year.

    2. Ownership Tax Year ▶ ☐ I represent that shareholders (as described in section 5.06 of Rev. Proc. 2002-38) holding more than half of the shares of the stock (as of the first day of the tax year to which the request relates) of the corporation have the same tax year or are concurrently changing to the tax year that the corporation adopts, retains, or changes to per item I, Part I, and that such tax year satisfies the requirement of section 4.01(3) of Rev. Proc. 2002-38. I also represent that the corporation is not precluded by section 4.02 of Rev. Proc. 2002-38 from obtaining automatic approval of such adoption, retention, or change in tax year.

Note: *If you do not use item P and the corporation wants a fiscal tax year, complete either item Q or R below. Item Q is used to request a fiscal tax year based on a business purpose and to make a back-up section 444 election. Item R is used to make a regular section 444 election.*

Q   Business Purpose- To request a fiscal tax year based on a business purpose, you must check box Q1. See instructions for details including payment of a user fee. You may also check box Q2 and/or box Q3.

    1. Check here ▶ ☐ if the fiscal year entered in item I, Part I, is requested under the prior approval provisions of Rev. Proc. 2002-39, 2002-22 I.R.B. 1046. Attach to Form 2553 a statement describing the relevant facts and circumstances and, if applicable, the gross receipts from sales and services necessary to establish a business purpose. See the instructions for details regarding the gross receipts from sales and services. If the IRS proposes to disapprove the requested fiscal year, do you want a conference with the IRS National Office?
    ☐ Yes   ☐ No

    2. Check here ▶ ☐ to show that the corporation intends to make a back-up section 444 election in the event the corporation's business purpose request is not approved by the IRS. (See instructions for more information.)

    3. Check here ▶ ☐ to show that the corporation agrees to adopt or change to a tax year ending December 31 if necessary for the IRS to accept this election for S corporation status in the event (1) the corporation's business purpose request is not approved and the corporation makes a back-up section 444 election, but is ultimately not qualified to make a section 444 election, or (2) the corporation's business purpose request is not approved and the corporation did not make a back-up section 444 election.

R   Section 444 Election- To make a section 444 election, you must check box R1 and you may also check box R2.

    1. Check here ▶ ☐ to show the corporation will make, if qualified, a section 444 election to have the fiscal tax year shown in item I, Part I. To make the election, you must complete **Form 8716,** Election To Have a Tax Year Other Than a Required Tax Year, and either attach it to Form 2553 or file it separately.

    2. Check here ▶ ☐ to show that the corporation agrees to adopt or change to a tax year ending December 31 if necessary for the IRS to accept this election for S corporation status in the event the corporation is ultimately not qualified to make a section 444 election.

Part III   Qualified Subchapter S Trust (QSST) Election Under Section 1361(d)(2)*

Income beneficiary's name and address	Social security number
Trust's name and address	Employer identification number

Date on which stock of the corporation was transferred to the trust (month, day, year)   . . . . ▶   /   /

In order for the trust named above to be a QSST and thus a qualifying shareholder of the S corporation for which this Form 2553 is filed, I hereby make the election under section 1361(d)(2). Under penalties of perjury, I certify that the trust meets the definitional requirements of section 1361(d)(3) and that all other information provided in Part III is true, correct, and complete.

_____   _____

Signature of income beneficiary or signature and title of legal representative or other qualified person making the election   Date

*Use Part III to make the QSST election only if stock of the corporation has been transferred to the trust on or before the date on which the corporation makes its election to be an S corporation. The QSST election must be made and filed separately if stock of the corporation is transferred to the trust after the date on which the corporation makes the S election.

                                ✳   Form **2553** (Rev. 12-2002)

Instructions for Form 2553

(Rev. December 2002)

Department of the Treasury
Internal Revenue Service

Election by a Small Business Corporation
Section references are to the Internal Revenue Code unless otherwise noted.

General Instructions

Purpose

To elect to be an S corporation, a corporation must file Form 2553. The election permits the income of the S corporation to be taxed to the shareholders of the corporation rather than to the corporation itself, except as noted below under **Taxes an S Corporation May Owe.**

Who May Elect

A corporation may elect to be an S corporation only if it meets all of the following tests:

1. It is a domestic corporation.

Note: *A limited liability company (LLC)* **must** *file* **Form 8832**, *Entity Classification Election, to elect to be treated as an association taxable as a corporation in order to elect to be an S corporation.*

2. It has no more than 75 shareholders. A husband and wife (and their estates) are treated as one shareholder for this requirement. All other persons are treated as separate shareholders.

3. Its only shareholders are individuals, estates, exempt organizations described in section 401(a) or 501(c)(3), or certain trusts described in section 1361(c)(2)(A). See the instructions for Part III regarding qualified subchapter S trusts (QSSTs).

A trustee of a trust wanting to make an election under section 1361(e)(3) to be an electing small business trust (ESBT) should see Notice 97-12, 1997-1 C.B. 385. However, in general, for tax years beginning after May 13, 2002, Notice 97-12 is superseded by Regulations section 1.1361-1(c)(1). Also see Rev. Proc. 98-23, 1998-1 C.B. 662, for guidance on how to convert a QSST to an ESBT. However, in general, for tax years beginning after May 13, 2002, Rev. Proc. 98-23 is superseded by Regulations section 1.1361-1(j)(12). If there was an inadvertent failure to timely file an ESBT election, see the relief provisions under Rev. Proc. 98-55, 1998-2 C.B. 643.

4. It has no nonresident alien shareholders.

5. It has only one class of stock (disregarding differences in voting rights). Generally, a corporation is treated as having only one class of stock if all outstanding shares of the corporation's stock confer identical rights to distribution and liquidation proceeds. See Regulations section 1.1361-1(l) for details.

6. It is not one of the following ineligible corporations:

a. A bank or thrift institution that uses the reserve method of accounting for bad debts under section 585,

b. An insurance company subject to tax under the rules of subchapter L of the Code,

c. A corporation that has elected to be treated as a possessions corporation under section 936, or

d. A domestic international sales corporation (DISC) or former DISC.

7. It has a permitted tax year as required by section 1378 or makes a section 444 election to have a tax year other than a permitted tax year. Section 1378 defines a permitted tax year as a tax year ending December 31, or any other tax year for which the corporation establishes a business purpose to the satisfaction of the IRS. See Part II for details on requesting a fiscal tax year based on a business purpose or on making a section 444 election.

8. Each shareholder consents as explained in the instructions for column K.

See sections 1361, 1362, and 1378 for additional information on the above tests.

A parent S corporation can elect to treat an eligible wholly-owned subsidiary as a qualified subchapter S subsidiary (QSub). If the election is made, the assets, liabilities, and items of income, deduction, and credit of the QSub are treated as those of the parent. To make the election, get **Form 8869**, Qualified Subchapter S Subsidiary Election. If the QSub election was not timely filed, the corporation may be entitled to relief under Rev. Proc. 98-55.

Taxes an S Corporation May Owe

An S corporation may owe income tax in the following instances:

1. If, at the end of any tax year, the corporation had accumulated earnings and profits, and its passive investment income under section 1362(d)(3) is more than 25% of its gross receipts, the corporation may owe tax on its excess net passive income.

2. A corporation with net recognized built-in gain (as defined in section 1374(d)(2)) may owe tax on its built-in gains.

3. A corporation that claimed investment credit before its first year as an S corporation will be liable for any investment credit recapture tax.

4. A corporation that used the LIFO inventory method for the year immediately preceding its first year as an S corporation may owe an additional tax due to LIFO recapture. The tax is paid in four equal installments, the first of which must be paid by the due date (not including extensions) of the corporation's income tax return for its last tax year as a C corporation.

For more details on these taxes, see the Instructions for Form 1120S.

Cat. No. 49978N

Where To File

Send the original election (no photocopies) or fax it to the Internal Revenue Service Center listed below. If the corporation files this election by fax, keep the original Form 2553 with the corporation's permanent records.

If the corporation's principal business, office, or agency is located in ▼	Use the following Internal Revenue Service Center address or fax number ▼
Connecticut, Delaware, District of Columbia, Illinois, Indiana, Kentucky, Maine, Maryland, Massachusetts, Michigan, New Hampshire, New Jersey, New York, North Carolina, Ohio, Pennsylvania, Rhode Island, South Carolina, Vermont, Virginia, West Virginia, Wisconsin	Cincinnati, OH 45999 (859) 669-5748
Alabama, Alaska, Arizona, Arkansas, California, Colorado, Florida, Georgia, Hawaii, Idaho, Iowa, Kansas, Louisiana, Minnesota, Mississippi, Missouri, Montana, Nebraska, Nevada, New Mexico, North Dakota, Oklahoma, Oregon, South Dakota, Tennessee, Texas, Utah, Washington, Wyoming	Ogden, UT 84201 (801) 620-7116

When To Make the Election

Complete and file Form 2553 **(a)** at any time before the 16th day of the 3rd month of the tax year, if filed during the tax year the election is to take effect, or **(b)** at any time during the preceding tax year. An election made no later than 2 months and 15 days after the beginning of a tax year that is less than 2½ months long is treated as timely made for that tax year. **An election made after the 15th day of the 3rd month but before the end of the tax year is effective for the next year.** For example, if a calendar tax year corporation makes the election in April 2002, it is effective for the corporation's 2003 calendar tax year.

However, an election made after the due date will be accepted as timely filed if the corporation can show that the failure to file on time was due to reasonable cause. To request relief for a late election, the corporation generally must request a private letter ruling and pay a user fee in accordance with Rev. Proc. 2002-1, 2002-1 I.R.B. 1 (or its successor). But if the election is filed within 12 months of its due date and the original due date for filing the corporation's initial Form 1120S has not passed, the ruling and user fee requirements do not apply. To request relief in this case, write "FILED PURSUANT TO REV. PROC. 98-55" at the top of page 1 of Form 2553, attach a statement explaining the reason for failing to file the election on time, and file Form 2553 as otherwise instructed. See Rev. Proc. 98-55 for more details.

See Regulations section 1.1362-6(b)(3)(iii) for how to obtain relief for an inadvertent invalid election if the corporation filed a timely election, but one or more shareholders did not file a timely consent.

Acceptance or Nonacceptance of Election

The service center will notify the corporation if its election is accepted and when it will take effect. The corporation will also be notified if its election is not accepted. The corporation should generally receive a determination on its election within 60 days after it has filed Form 2553. If box Q1 in Part II is checked on page 2, the corporation will receive a ruling letter from the IRS in Washington, DC, that either approves or denies the selected tax year. When box Q1 is checked, it will generally take an additional 90 days for the Form 2553 to be accepted.

Care should be exercised to ensure that the IRS receives the election. If the corporation is not notified of acceptance or nonacceptance of its election within 3 months of the date of filing (date mailed), or within 6 months if box Q1 is checked, take follow-up action by corresponding with the service center where the corporation filed the election.

If the IRS questions whether Form 2553 was filed, an acceptable proof of filing is **(a)** certified or registered mail receipt (timely postmarked) from the U.S. Postal Service, or its equivalent from a designated private delivery service (see Notice 2002-62, 2002-39 I.R.B. 574 (or its successor)); **(b)** Form 2553 with accepted stamp; **(c)** Form 2553 with stamped IRS received date; or **(d)** IRS letter stating that Form 2553 has been accepted.

⚠ CAUTION — *Do not file Form 1120S for any tax year before the year the election takes effect. If the corporation is now required to file **Form 1120,** U.S. Corporation Income Tax Return, or any other applicable tax return, continue filing it until the election takes effect.*

End of Election

Once the election is made, it stays in effect until it is terminated. If the election is terminated in a tax year beginning after 1996, IRS consent is generally required for another election by the corporation (or a successor corporation) on Form 2553 for any tax year before the 5th tax year after the first tax year in which the termination took effect. See Regulations section 1.1362-5 for details.

Specific Instructions

Part I (*All corporations must complete.*)

Name and Address of Corporation

Enter the true corporate name as stated in the corporate charter or other legal document creating it. If the corporation's mailing address is the same as someone else's, such as a shareholder's, enter "c/o" and this person's name following the name of the corporation. Include the suite, room, or other unit number after the street address. If the Post Office does not deliver to the street address and the corporation has a P.O. box, show the box number instead of the street address. If the corporation changed its name or address after applying for its employer identification number, be sure to check the box in item D of Part I.

Item A. Employer Identification Number (EIN)

If the corporation has applied for an EIN but has not received it, enter "applied for." If the corporation does not have an EIN, it should apply for one on **Form SS-4,** Application for Employer Identification Number. You can order Form SS-4 by calling 1-800-TAX-FORM (1-800-829-3676) or by accessing the IRS Web Site **www.irs.gov.**

Item E. Effective Date of Election

Enter the beginning effective date (month, day, year) of the tax year requested for the S corporation. Generally, this will be the beginning date of the tax year for which the ending effective date is required to be shown in item I, Part I. For a new corporation (first year the corporation exists) it will generally be the date required to be shown in item H, Part I. The tax year of a new corporation starts on the date that it has shareholders, acquires assets, or begins doing business, whichever happens first. If the effective date for item E for a newly formed corporation is later than the date in item H, the corporation should file Form 1120 or Form 1120-A for the tax period between these dates.

Column K. Shareholders' Consent Statement

Each shareholder who owns (or is deemed to own) stock at the time the election is made must consent to the election. If the election is made during the corporation's tax year for which it first takes effect, any person who held stock at any time during the part of that year that occurs before the election is made, must consent to the election, even though the person may have sold or transferred his or her stock before the election is made.

An election made during the first 2½ months of the tax year is effective for the following tax year if any person who held stock in the corporation during the part of the tax year before the election was made, and who did not hold stock at the time the election was made, did not consent to the election.

Note: *Once the election is made, a new shareholder is not required to consent to the election; a new Form 2553 will not be required.*

Each shareholder consents by signing and dating in column K or signing and dating a separate consent statement described below. The following special rules apply in determining who must sign the consent statement.

• If a husband and wife have a community interest in the stock or in the income from it, both must consent.

• Each tenant in common, joint tenant, and tenant by the entirety must consent.

• A minor's consent is made by the minor, legal representative of the minor, or a natural or adoptive parent of the minor if no legal representative has been appointed.

• The consent of an estate is made by the executor or administrator.

• The consent of an electing small business trust is made by the trustee.

• If the stock is owned by a trust (other than an electing small business trust), the deemed owner of the trust must consent. See section 1361(c)(2) for details regarding trusts that are permitted to be shareholders and rules for determining who is the deemed owner.

Continuation sheet or separate consent statement. If you need a continuation sheet or use a separate consent statement, attach it to Form 2553. The separate consent statement must contain the name, address, and EIN of the corporation and the shareholder information requested in columns J through N of Part I. If you want, you may combine all the shareholders' consents in one statement.

Column L

Enter the number of shares of stock each shareholder owns and the dates the stock was acquired. If the election is made during the corporation's tax year for which it first takes effect, do not list the shares of stock for those shareholders who sold or transferred all of their stock before the election was made. However, these shareholders must still consent to the election for it to be effective for the tax year.

Column M

Enter the social security number of each shareholder who is an individual. Enter the EIN of each shareholder that is an estate, a qualified trust, or an exempt organization.

Column N

Enter the month and day that each shareholder's tax year ends. If a shareholder is changing his or her tax year, enter the tax year the shareholder is changing to, and attach an explanation indicating the present tax year and the basis for the change (e.g., automatic revenue procedure or letter ruling request).

Signature

Form 2553 must be signed by the president, treasurer, assistant treasurer, chief accounting officer, or other corporate officer (such as tax officer) authorized to sign.

Part II

Complete Part II if you selected a tax year ending on any date other than December 31 (other than a 52-53-week tax year ending with reference to the month of December).

Note: *In certain circumstances the corporation may not obtain automatic approval of a fiscal year under the natural business year (Box P1) or ownership tax year (Box P2) provisions if it is under examination, before an area office, or before a federal court with respect to any income tax issue and the annual accounting period is under consideration. For details, see section 4.02 of Rev. Proc. 2002-38, 2002-22 I.R.B. 1037.*

Box P1

Attach a statement showing separately for each month the amount of gross receipts for the most recent 47 months. A corporation that does not have a 47-month period of gross receipts cannot automatically establish a natural business year.

Box Q1

For examples of an acceptable business purpose for requesting a fiscal tax year, see section 5.02 of Rev. Proc. 2002-39, 2002-22 I.R.B. 1046, and Rev. Rul. 87-57, 1987-2 C.B. 117.

Attach a statement showing the relevant facts and circumstances to establish a business purpose for the requested fiscal year. For details on what is sufficient to establish a business purpose, see section 5.02 of Rev. Proc. 2002-39.

If your business purpose is based on one of the natural business year tests provided in section 5.03 of Rev. Proc. 2002-39, identify if you are using the 25% gross receipts, annual business cycle, or seasonal business test. For the 25% gross receipts test, provide a schedule showing the amount of gross receipts for each month for the most recent 47 months. For either the annual business cycle or seasonal business test, provide the gross receipts from sales and services (and inventory costs, if applicable) for each month of the short period, if any, and the three immediately preceding tax years. If the corporation has been in existence for less than three tax years, submit figures for the period of existence.

If you check box Q1, you will be charged a user fee of up to $600 (subject to change—see Rev. Proc. 2002-1 or its successor). Do not pay the fee when filing Form 2553. The service center will send Form 2553 to the IRS in Washington, DC, who, in turn, will notify the corporation that the fee is due.

Box Q2

If the corporation makes a back-up section 444 election for which it is qualified, then the election will take effect in the event the business purpose request is not approved. In some cases, the tax year requested under the back-up section 444 election may be different than the tax year requested under business purpose. See **Form 8716,** Election To Have a Tax Year Other Than a Required Tax Year, for details on making a back-up section 444 election.

Boxes Q2 and R2

If the corporation is not qualified to make the section 444 election after making the item Q2 back-up section 444 election or indicating its intention to make the election in item R1, and therefore it later files a calendar year return, it should write "Section 444 Election Not Made" in the top left corner of the first calendar year Form 1120S it files.

Part III

Certain qualified subchapter S trusts (QSSTs) may make the QSST election required by section 1361(d)(2) in Part III. Part III may be used to make the QSST election only if corporate stock has been transferred to the trust on or before the date on which the corporation makes its election to be an S corporation. However, a statement can be used instead of Part III to make the election. If there was an inadvertent failure to timely file a QSST election, see the relief provisions under Rev. Proc. 98-55.

Note: *Use Part III **only** if you make the election in Part I (i.e., Form 2553 cannot be filed with only Part III completed).*

The deemed owner of the QSST must also consent to the S corporation election in column K, page 1, of Form 2553. See section 1361(c)(2).

Paperwork Reduction Act Notice. We ask for the information on this form to carry out the Internal Revenue laws of the United States. You are required to give us the information. We need it to ensure that you are complying with these laws and to allow us to figure and collect the right amount of tax.

You are not required to provide the information requested on a form that is subject to the Paperwork Reduction Act unless the form displays a valid OMB control number. Books or records relating to a form or its instructions must be retained as long as their contents may become material in the administration of any Internal Revenue law. Generally, tax returns and return information are confidential, as required by section 6103.

The time needed to complete and file this form will depend on individual circumstances. The estimated average time is:

Recordkeeping	9 hr., 34 min.
Learning about the law or the form	3 hr., 28 min.
Preparing, copying, assembling, and sending the form to the IRS	3 hr., 47 min.

If you have comments concerning the accuracy of these time estimates or suggestions for making this form simpler, we would be happy to hear from you. You can write to the Tax Forms Committee, Western Area Distribution Center, Rancho Cordova, CA 95743-0001. **Do not** send the form to this address. Instead, see **Where To File** on page 2.

Form **SS-8**

(Rev. January 2001)
Department of the Treasury
Internal Revenue Service

Determination of Worker Status for Purposes of Federal Employment Taxes and Income Tax Withholding

OMB No. 1545-0004

Name of firm (or person) for whom the worker performed services	Worker's name

Firm's address (include street address, apt. or suite no., city, state, and ZIP code)	Worker's address (include street address, apt. or suite no., city, state, and ZIP code)

Trade name	Telephone number (include area code) ( )	Worker's social security number

Telephone number (include area code) ( )	Firm's employer identification number	Worker's employer identification number (if any)

Important Information Needed To Process Your Request

If this form is being completed by the worker, the IRS must have your permission to disclose your name to the firm. Do you object to disclosing your name and the information on this form to the firm? . . . . ☐ **Yes** ☐ **No**

If you answered "Yes" or did not check a box, stop here. The IRS cannot act on your request and a determination will not be issued.

You must answer ALL items OR mark them "Unknown" or "Does not apply." If you need more space, attach another sheet.

A This form is being completed by: ☐ Firm ☐ Worker; for services performed _____ to _____ .
(beginning date) (ending date)

B Explain your reason(s) for filing this form (e.g., you received a bill from the IRS, you believe you received a Form 1099 or Form W-2 erroneously, you are unable to get worker's compensation benefits, you were audited or are being audited by the IRS). --------------------
----

C Total number of workers who performed or are performing the same or similar services _____ .

D How did the worker obtain the job? ☐ Application ☐ Bid ☐ Employment Agency ☐ Other (specify) _____

E Attach copies of all supporting documentation (contracts, invoices, memos, Forms W-2, Forms 1099, IRS closing agreements, IRS rulings, etc.). In addition, please inform us of any current or past litigation concerning the worker's status. If no income reporting forms (Form 1099-MISC or W-2) were furnished to the worker, enter the amount of income earned for the year(s) at issue $ _____ .

F Describe the firm's business. --

G Describe the work done by the worker and provide the worker's job title. --------------------------------------
----

H Explain why you believe the worker is an employee or an independent contractor. --------------------------------
----

I Did the worker perform services for the firm before getting this position? . . . . ☐ Yes ☐ No ☐ N/A
If "Yes," what were the dates of the prior service? --
If "Yes," explain the differences, if any, between the current and prior service. --------------------------------
----

J If the work is done under a written agreement between the firm and the worker, attach a copy (preferably signed by both parties). Describe the terms and conditions of the work arrangement. --

For Privacy Act and Paperwork Reduction Act Notice, see page 5.   Cat. No. 16106T   Form **SS-8** (Rev. 1-2001)

Part I   Behavioral Control

1   What specific training and/or instruction is the worker given by the firm? ....

2   How does the worker receive work assignments? ....

3   Who determines the methods by which the assignments are performed? ....

4   Who is the worker required to contact if problems or complaints arise and who is responsible for their resolution? ....

5   What types of reports are required from the worker? Attach examples. ....

6   Describe the worker's daily routine (i.e., schedule, hours, etc.). ....

7   At what location(s) does the worker perform services (e.g., firm's premises, own shop or office, home, customer's location, etc.)? ....

8   Describe any meetings the worker is required to attend and any penalties for not attending (e.g., sales meetings, monthly meetings, staff meetings, etc.). ....

9   Is the worker required to provide the services personally? . . . . □ Yes   □ No

10 If substitutes or helpers are needed, who hires them? ....

11 If the worker hires the substitutes or helpers, is approval required? . . . . □ Yes   □ No
    If "Yes," by whom? ....

12 Who pays the substitutes or helpers? ....

13 Is the worker reimbursed if the worker pays the substitutes or helpers? . . . . □ Yes   □ No
    If "Yes," by whom? ....

Part II   Financial Control

1   List the supplies, equipment, materials, and property provided by each party:
    The firm ....
    The worker ....
    Other party ....

2   Does the worker lease equipment? . . . . □ Yes   □ No
    If "Yes," what are the terms of the lease? (Attach a copy or explanatory statement.) ....

3   What expenses are incurred by the worker in the performance of services for the firm? ....

4   Specify which, if any, expenses are reimbursed by:
    The firm ....
    Other party ....

5   Type of pay the worker receives: □ Salary   □ Commission   □ Hourly Wage   □ Piece Work
    □ Lump Sum   □ Other (specify) ....
    If type of pay is commission, and the firm guarantees a minimum amount of pay, specify amount $ _____ .

6   If the worker is paid by a firm other than the one listed on this form for these services, enter name, address, and employer identification number of the payer. ....

7   Is the worker allowed a drawing account for advances? . . . . □ Yes   □ No
    If "Yes," how often? ....
    Specify any restrictions. ....

8   Whom does the customer pay? . . . . □ Firm   □ Worker
    If worker, does the worker pay the total amount to the firm? □ Yes   □ No   If "No," explain. ....

9   Does the firm carry worker's compensation insurance on the worker? . . . . □ Yes   □ No

10 What economic loss or financial risk, if any, can the worker incur beyond the normal loss of salary (e.g., loss or damage of equipment, material, etc.)? ....

Form SS-8 (Rev. 1-2001)   Page **3**

Part III   Relationship of the Worker and Firm

1   List the benefits available to the worker (e.g., paid vacations, sick pay, pensions, bonuses). ----------------------------------
    ----

2   Can the relationship be terminated by either party without incurring liability or penalty? . . . . ☐ Yes ☐ No
    If "No," explain your answer. --
    ----

3   Does the worker perform similar services for others? . . . . ☐ Yes ☐ No
    If "Yes," is the worker required to get approval from the firm? . . . . ☐ Yes ☐ No

4   Describe any agreements prohibiting competition between the worker and the firm while the worker is performing services or during any later
    period. Attach any available documentation. ---

5   Is the worker a member of a union? . . . . ☐ Yes ☐ No

6   What type of advertising, if any, does the worker do (e.g., a business listing in a directory, business cards, etc.)? Provide copies, if applicable.
    ----

7   If the worker assembles or processes a product at home, who provides the materials and instructions or pattern? ----------------
    ----

8   What does the worker do with the finished product (e.g., return it to the firm, provide it to another party, or sell it)? ----------
    ----

9   How does the firm represent the worker to its customers (e.g., employee, partner, representative, or contractor)? ----------------
    ----

10 If the worker no longer performs services for the firm, how did the relationship end? ---
    ----

Part IV   For Service Providers or Salespersons- Complete this part if the worker provided a service directly to
              customers or is a salesperson.

1   What are the worker's responsibilities in soliciting new customers? ---
    ----

2   Who provides the worker with leads to prospective customers? ---

3   Describe any reporting requirements pertaining to the leads. --
    ----

4   What terms and conditions of sale, if any, are required by the firm? ---

5   Are orders submitted to and subject to approval by the firm? . . . . ☐ Yes ☐ No

6   Who determines the worker's territory? --

7   Did the worker pay for the privilege of serving customers on the route or in the territory? . . . . ☐ Yes ☐ No
    If "Yes," whom did the worker pay? --
    If "Yes," how much did the worker pay? . . . . $ _____

8   Where does the worker sell the product (e.g., in a home, retail establishment, etc.)? --
    ----

9   List the product and/or services distributed by the worker (e.g., meat, vegetables, fruit, bakery products, beverages, or laundry or dry cleaning
    services). If more than one type of product and/or service is distributed, specify the principal one. -----------------------------
    ----

10 Does the worker sell life insurance full time? . . . . ☐ Yes ☐ No

11 Does the worker sell other types of insurance for the firm? . . . . ☐ Yes ☐ No
    If "Yes," enter the percentage of the worker's total working time spent in selling other types of insurance. . . . _____ %

12 If the worker solicits orders from wholesalers, retailers, contractors, or operators of hotels, restaurants, or other similar
    establishments, enter the percentage of the worker's time spent in the solicitation. . . . . _____ %

13 Is the merchandise purchased by the customers for resale or use in their business operations? . . . . ☐ Yes ☐ No
    Describe the merchandise and state whether it is equipment installed on the customers' premises. ----------------------------
    ----

Part V   Signature (see page 4)

Under penalties of perjury, I declare that I have examined this request, including accompanying documents, and to the best of my knowledge and belief, the facts
presented are true, correct, and complete.

Signature ▶ _____   Title ▶ _____   Date ▶ _____
                   (Type or print name below)

Form **SS-8** (Rev. 1-2001)

General Instructions

Section references are to the Internal Revenue Code unless otherwise noted.

Purpose

Firms and workers file Form SS-8 to request a determination of the status of a worker for purposes of Federal employment taxes and income tax withholding.

A Form SS-8 determination may be requested only in order to resolve Federal tax matters. The taxpayer requesting a determination must file an income tax return for the years under consideration before a determination can be issued. If Form SS-8 is submitted for a tax year for which the statute of limitations on the tax return has expired, a determination letter will not be issued. The statute of limitations expires 3 years from the due date of the tax return or the date filed, whichever is later.

The IRS does not issue a determination letter for proposed transactions or on hypothetical situations. We may, however, issue an information letter when it is considered appropriate.

Definition

Firm. For the purposes of this form, the term "firm" means any individual, business enterprise, organization, state, or other entity for which a worker has performed services. The firm may or may not have paid the worker directly for these services. **If the firm was not responsible for payment for services, please be sure to complete question 6 in Part II of Form SS-8.**

The SS-8 Determination Process

The IRS will acknowledge the receipt of your Form SS-8. Because there are usually two (or more) parties who could be affected by a determination of employment status, the IRS attempts to get information from all parties involved by sending those parties blank Forms SS-8 for completion. The case will be assigned to a technician who will review the facts, apply the law, and render a decision. The technician may ask for additional information before rendering a decision. The IRS will generally issue a formal determination to the firm or payer (if that is a different entity), and will send a copy to the worker. A determination letter applies only to a worker (or a class of workers) requesting it, and the decision is binding on the IRS. In certain cases, a formal determination will not be issued; instead, an information letter may be issued. Although an information letter is advisory only and is not binding on the IRS, it may be used to assist the worker to fulfill his or her Federal tax obligations. This process takes approximately 120 days.

Neither the SS-8 determination process nor the review of any records in connection with the determination constitutes an examination (audit) of any Federal tax return. If the periods under consideration have previously been examined, the SS-8 determination process will not constitute a reexamination under IRS reopening procedures. Because this is not an examination of any Federal tax return, the appeal rights available in connection with an examination do not apply to an SS-8 determination. However, if you disagree with a determination and you have additional information concerning the work relationship that you believe was not previously considered, you may request that the determining office reconsider the determination.

Completing Form SS-8

Please answer all questions as completely as possible. Attach additional sheets if you need more space. Provide information for all years the worker provided services for the firm. Determinations are based on the entire relationship between the firm and the worker.

Additional copies of this form may be obtained by calling 1-800-TAX-FORM (1-800-829-3676) or from the IRS Web Site at **www.irs.gov.**

Fee

There is no fee for requesting an SS-8 determination letter.

Signature

The Form SS-8 must be signed and dated by the taxpayer. A stamped signature will not be accepted.

The person who signs for a corporation must be an officer of the corporation who has personal knowledge of the facts. If the corporation is a member of an affiliated group filing a consolidated return, it must be signed by an officer of the common parent of the group.

The person signing for a trust, partnership, or limited liability company must be, respectively, a trustee, general partner, or member-manager who has personal knowledge of the facts.

Where To File

Send the completed Form SS-8 to the address listed below for the firm's location. However, for cases involving Federal agencies, send the form to the Internal Revenue Service, Attn: CC:CORP:T:C, Ben Franklin Station, P.O. Box 7604, Washington, DC 20044.

Firm's location:	Send to:
Alaska, Arizona, Arkansas, California, Colorado, Hawaii, Idaho, Illinois, Iowa, Kansas, Minnesota, Missouri, Montana, Nebraska, Nevada, New Mexico, North Dakota, Oklahoma, Oregon, South Dakota, Texas, Utah, Washington, Wisconsin, Wyoming, American Samoa, Guam, Puerto Rico, U.S. Virgin Islands	Internal Revenue Service SS-8 Determinations P.O. Box 1231 Stop 4106 AUCSC Austin, TX 78767
Alabama, Connecticut, Delaware, District of Columbia, Florida, Georgia, Indiana, Kentucky, Louisiana, Maine, Maryland, Massachusetts, Michigan, Mississippi, New Hampshire, New Jersey, New York, North Carolina, Ohio, Pennsylvania, Rhode Island, South Carolina, Tennessee, Vermont, Virginia, West Virginia, all other locations not listed	Internal Revenue Service SS-8 Determinations 40 Lakemont Road Newport, VT 05855-1555

Instructions for Workers

If you are requesting a determination for more than one firm, complete a separate Form SS-8 for each firm.

 Form SS-8 is not a claim for refund of social security and Medicare taxes or Federal income tax withholding.

If you are found to be an employee, you are responsible for filing an amended return for any corrections related to this decision. A determination that a worker is an employee does not necessarily reduce any current or prior tax liability. For more information, call 1-800-829-1040.

Time for filing a claim for refund. Generally, you must file your claim for a credit or refund within 3 years from the date your original return was filed or within 2 years from the date the tax was paid, whichever is later.

Form SS-8 does not prevent the expiration of the time in which a claim for a refund must be filed. If you are concerned about a refund, and the statute of limitations for filing a claim for refund for the year(s) at issue has not yet expired, you should file **Form 1040X,** Amended U.S. Individual Income Tax Return, to protect your statute of limitations. File a separate Form 1040X for each year.

On the Form 1040X you file, do not complete lines 1 through 24 on the form. Write "Protective Claim" at the top of the form, sign and date it. In addition, you should enter the following statement in Part II, Explanation of Changes to Income, Deductions, and Credits: "Filed Form SS-8 with the Internal Revenue Service Office in (Austin, TX; Newport, VT; or Washington, DC; as appropriate). By filing this protective claim, I reserve the right to file a claim for any refund that may be due after a determination of my employment tax status has been completed."

Filing Form SS-8 does not alter the requirement to timely file an income tax return. Do not delay filing your tax return in anticipation of an answer to your SS-8 request. You must file an income tax return for related tax years before a determination can be issued. In addition, if applicable, do not delay in responding to a request for payment while waiting for a determination of your worker status.

Instructions for Firms

If a **worker** has requested a determination of his or her status while working for you, you will receive a request from the IRS to complete a Form SS-8. In cases of this type, the IRS usually gives each party an opportunity to present a statement of the facts because any decision will affect the employment tax status of the parties. Failure to respond to this request will not prevent the IRS from issuing an information letter to the worker based on the information he or she has made available so that the worker may fulfill his or her Federal tax obligations. However, the information that you provide is extremely valuable in determining the status of the worker.

If **you** are requesting a determination for a particular class of worker, complete the form for **one** individual who is representative of the class of workers whose status is in question. If you want a written determination for more than one class of workers, complete a separate Form SS-8 for one worker from each class whose status is typical of that class. A written determination for any worker will apply to other workers of the same class if the facts are not materially different for these workers. Please provide a list of names and addresses of all workers potentially affected by this determination.

If you have a reasonable basis for not treating a worker as an employee, you may be relieved from having to pay employment taxes for that worker under section 530 of the 1978 Revenue Act. However, this relief provision cannot be considered in conjunction with a Form SS-8 determination because the determination does not constitute an examination of any tax return. For more information regarding section 530 of the 1978 Revenue Act and to determine if you qualify for relief under this section, you may visit the IRS Web Site at **www.irs.gov**.

Privacy Act and Paperwork Reduction Act Notice. We ask for the information on this form to carry out the Internal Revenue laws of the United States. This information will be used to determine the employment status of the worker(s) described on the form. Subtitle C, Employment Taxes, of the Internal Revenue Code imposes employment taxes on wages. Sections 3121(d), 3306(a), and 3401(c) and (d) and the related regulations define employee and employer for purposes of employment taxes imposed under Subtitle C. Section 6001 authorizes the IRS to request information needed to determine if a worker(s) or firm is subject to these taxes. Section 6109 requires you to provide your taxpayer identification number. Neither workers nor firms are required to request a status determination, but if you choose to do so, you must provide the information requested on this form. Failure to provide the requested information may prevent us from making a status determination. If any worker or the firm has requested a status determination, and you are being asked to provide information for use in that determination, you are not required to provide the requested information. However, failure to provide such information will prevent the IRS from considering it in making the status determination. Providing false or fraudulent information may subject you to penalties. Routine uses of this information include providing it to the Department of Justice for use in civil and criminal litigation, to the Social Security Administration for the administration of social security programs, and to cities, states, and the District of Columbia for the administration of their tax laws. We may also provide this information to the affected worker(s) or the firm as part of the status determination process.

You are not required to provide the information requested on a form that is subject to the Paperwork Reduction Act unless the form displays a valid OMB control number. Books or records relating to a form or its instructions must be retained as long as their contents may become material in the administration of any Internal Revenue law. Generally, tax returns and return information are confidential, as required by section 6103.

The time needed to complete and file this form will vary depending on individual circumstances. The estimated average time is: **Recordkeeping,** 22 hrs.; **Learning about the law or the form,** 47 min.; and **Preparing and sending the form to the IRS,** 1 hr., 11 min. If you have comments concerning the accuracy of these time estimates or suggestions for making this form simpler, we would be happy to hear from you. You can write to the Tax Forms Committee, Western Area Distribution Center, Rancho Cordova, CA 95743-0001. **Do not** send the tax form to this address. Instead, see **Where To File** on page 4.

UCC FINANCING STATEMENT

FOLLOW INSTRUCTIONS (front and back) CAREFULLY

A. NAME & PHONE OF CONTACT AT FILER [optional]

B. SEND ACKNOWLEDGMENT TO: (Name and Address)

THE ABOVE SPACE IS FOR FILING OFFICE USE ONLY

1. DEBTOR'S EXACT FULL LEGAL NAME - insert only one debtor name (1a or 1b) - do not abbreviate or combine names

1a. ORGANIZATION'S NAME			
OR 1b. INDIVIDUAL'S LAST NAME	FIRST NAME	MIDDLE NAME	SUFFIX
1c. MAILING ADDRESS	CITY	STATE	POSTAL CODE	COUNTRY

| 1d. TAX ID #: SSN OR EIN | ADD'L INFO RE ORGANIZATION DEBTOR | 1e. TYPE OF ORGANIZATION | 1f. JURISDICTION OF ORGANIZATION | 1g. ORGANIZATIONAL ID #, if any | NONE |

2. ADDITIONAL DEBTOR'S EXACT FULL LEGAL NAME - insert only one debtor name (2a or 2b) - do not abbreviate or combine names

2a. ORGANIZATION'S NAME			
OR 2b. INDIVIDUAL'S LAST NAME	FIRST NAME	MIDDLE NAME	SUFFIX
2c. MAILING ADDRESS	CITY	STATE	POSTAL CODE	COUNTRY

| 2d. TAX ID #: SSN OR EIN | ADD'L INFO RE ORGANIZATION DEBTOR | 2e. TYPE OF ORGANIZATION | 2f. JURISDICTION OF ORGANIZATION | 2g. ORGANIZATIONAL ID #, if any | NONE |

3. SECURED PARTY'S NAME (or NAME of TOTAL ASSIGNEE of ASSIGNOR S/P) - insert only one secured party name (3a or 3b)

3a. ORGANIZATION'S NAME			
OR 3b. INDIVIDUAL'S LAST NAME	FIRST NAME	MIDDLE NAME	SUFFIX
3c. MAILING ADDRESS	CITY	STATE	POSTAL CODE	COUNTRY

4. This FINANCING STATEMENT covers the following collateral:

| 5. ALTERNATIVE DESIGNATION [if applicable]: | LESSEE/LESSOR | CONSIGNEE/CONSIGNOR | BAILEE/BAILOR | SELLER/BUYER | AG. LIEN | NON-UCC FILING |

| 6. This FINANCING STATEMENT is to be filed [for record] (or recorded) in the REAL ESTATE RECORDS. Attach Addendum [if applicable] | 7. Check to REQUEST SEARCH REPORT(S) on Debtor(s) [ADDITIONAL FEE] [optional] | All Debtors | Debtor 1 | Debtor 2 |

8. OPTIONAL FILER REFERENCE DATA

FILING OFFICE COPY — NATIONAL UCC FINANCING STATEMENT (FORM UCC1) (REV. 07/29/98)

UCC FINANCING STATEMENT ADDENDUM

FOLLOW INSTRUCTIONS (front and back) CAREFULLY

9. NAME OF FIRST DEBTOR (1a or 1b) ON RELATED FINANCING STATEMENT

	9a. ORGANIZATION'S NAME		
OR	9b. INDIVIDUAL'S LAST NAME	FIRST NAME	MIDDLE NAME,SUFFIX

10. MISCELLANEOUS:

THE ABOVE SPACE IS FOR FILING OFFICE USE ONLY

11. ADDITIONAL DEBTOR'S EXACT FULL LEGAL NAME - insert only <u>one</u> name (11a or 11b) - do not abbreviate or combine names

	11a. ORGANIZATION'S NAME				
OR	11b. INDIVIDUAL'S LAST NAME	FIRST NAME	MIDDLE NAME		SUFFIX

11c. MAILING ADDRESS	CITY	STATE	POSTAL CODE	COUNTRY

11d. TAX ID #: SSN OR EIN	ADD'L INFO RE ORGANIZATION DEBTOR	11e. TYPE OF ORGANIZATION	11f. JURISDICTION OF ORGANIZATION	11g. ORGANIZATIONAL ID #. if any	NONE

12. ☐ ADDITIONAL SECURED PARTY'S or ☐ ASSIGNOR S/P'S NAME - insert only <u>one</u> name (12a or 12b)

	12a. ORGANIZATION'S NAME				
OR	12b. INDIVIDUAL'S LAST NAME	FIRST NAME	MIDDLE NAME		SUFFIX

12c. MAILING ADDRESS	CITY	STATE	POSTAL CODE	COUNTRY

13. This FINANCING STATEMENT covers ☐ timber to be cut or ☐ as-extracted collateral, or is filed as a ☐ fixture filing.

14. Description of real estate:

15. Name and address of a RECORD OWNER of above-described real estate (if Debtor does not have a record interest):

16. Additional collateral description:

17. Check <u>only</u> if applicable and check <u>only</u> one box.

Debtor is a ☐ Trust or ☐ Trustee acting with respect to property held in trust or ☐ Decedent's Estate

18. Check <u>only</u> if applicable and check <u>only</u> one box.

☐ Debtor is a TRANSMITTING UTILITY

☐ Filed in connection with a Manufactured-Home Transaction — effective 30 years

☐ Filed in connection with a Public-Finance Transaction — effective 30 years

FILING OFFICE COPY — NATIONAL UCC FINANCING STATEMENT ADDENDUM (FORM UCC1Ad) (REV. 07/29/98)

Instructions for National UCC Financing Statement (Form UCC1)

Please type or laser-print this form. Be sure it is completely legible. Read all Instructions, especially Instruction 1; correct Debtor name is crucial. Follow Instructions completely.

Fill in form very carefully; mistakes may have important legal consequences. If you have questions, consult your attorney. Filing office cannot give legal advice.

Do not insert anything in the open space in the upper portion of this form; it is reserved for filing office use.

When properly completed, send Filing Office Copy, with required fee, to filing office. If you want an acknowledgment, complete item B and, if filing in a filing office that returns an acknowledgment copy furnished by filer, you may also send Acknowledgment Copy; otherwise detach. If you want to make a search request, complete item 7 (after reading Instruction 7 below) and send Search Report Copy, otherwise detach. Always detach Debtor and Secured Party Copies.

If you need to use attachments, use 8-1/2 X 11 inch sheets and put at the top of each sheet the name of the first Debtor, formatted exactly as it appears in item 1 of this form; you are encouraged to use Addendum (Form UCC1Ad).

A. To assist filing offices that might wish to communicate with filer, filer may provide information in item A. This item is optional.

B. Complete item B if you want an acknowledgment sent to you. If filing in a filing office that returns an acknowledgment copy furnished by filer, present simultaneously with this form a carbon or other copy of this form for use as an acknowledgment copy.

1. **Debtor name**: Enter only one Debtor name in item 1, an organization's name (1a) or an individual's name (1b). Enter Debtor's exact full legal name. Don't abbreviate.

1a. Organization Debtor. "Organization" means an entity having a legal identity separate from its owner. A partnership is an organization; a sole proprietorship is not an organization, even if it does business under a trade name. If Debtor is a partnership, enter exact full legal name of partnership; you need not enter names of partners as additional Debtors. If Debtor is a registered organization (e.g., corporation, limited partnership, limited liability company), it is advisable to examine Debtor's current filed charter documents to determine Debtor's correct name, organization type, and jurisdiction of organization.

1b. Individual Debtor. "Individual" means a natural person; this includes a sole proprietorship, whether or not operating under a trade name. Don't use prefixes (Mr., Mrs., Ms.). Use suffix box only for titles of lineage (Jr., Sr., III) and not for other suffixes or titles (e.g., M.D.). Use married woman's personal name (Mary Smith, not Mrs. John Smith). Enter individual Debtor's family name (surname) in Last Name box, first given name in First Name box, and all additional given names in Middle Name box.

For both organization and individual Debtors: Don't use Debtor's trade name, DBA, AKA, FKA, Division name, etc. in place of or combined with Debtor's legal name; you may add such other names as additional Debtors if you wish (but this is neither required nor recommended).

1c. An address is always required for the Debtor named in 1a or 1b.

1d. Debtor's taxpayer identification number (tax ID #) — social security number or employer identification number — may be required in some states.

1e,f,g. "Additional information re organization Debtor" is always required. Type of organization and jurisdiction of organization as well as Debtor's exact legal name can be determined from Debtor's current filed charter document. Organizational ID #, if any, is assigned by the agency where the charter document was filed; this is different from tax ID #; this should be entered preceded by the 2-character U.S. Postal identification of state of organization if one of the United States (e.g., CA12345, for a California corporation whose organizational ID # is 12345); if agency does not assign organizational ID #, check box in item 1g indicating "none."

Note: If Debtor is a trust or a trustee acting with respect to property held in trust, enter Debtor's name in item 1 and attach Addendum (Form UCC1Ad) and check appropriate box in item 17. If Debtor is a decedent's estate, enter name of deceased individual in item 1b and attach Addendum (Form UCC1Ad) and check appropriate box in item 17. If Debtor is a transmitting utility or this Financing Statement is filed in connection with a Manufactured-Home Transaction or a Public-Finance Transaction as defined in applicable Commercial Code, attach Addendum (Form UCC1Ad) and check appropriate box in item 18.

2. If an additional Debtor is included, complete item 2, determined and formatted per Instruction 1. To include further additional Debtors, or one or more additional Secured Parties, attach either Addendum (Form UCC1Ad) or other additional page(s), using correct name format. Follow Instruction 1 for determining and formatting additional names.

3. Enter information for Secured Party or Total Assignee, determined and formatted per Instruction 1. If there is more than one Secured Party, see Instruction 2. If there has been a total assignment of the Secured Party's interest prior to filing this form, you may either (1) enter Assignor S/P's name and address in item 3 and file an Amendment (Form UCC3) [see item 5 of that form]; or (2) enter Total Assignee's name and address in item 3 and, if you wish, also attaching Addendum (Form UCC1Ad) giving Assignor S/P's name and address in item 12.

4. Use item 4 to indicate the collateral covered by this Financing Statement. If space in item 4 is insufficient, put the entire collateral description or continuation of the collateral description on either Addendum (Form UCC1Ad) or other attached additional page(s).

5. If filer desires (at filer's option) to use titles of lessee and lessor, or consignee and consignor, or seller and buyer (in the case of accounts or chattel paper), or bailee and bailor instead of Debtor and Secured Party, check the appropriate box in item 5. If this is an agricultural lien (as defined in applicable Commercial Code) filing or is otherwise not a UCC security interest filing (e.g., a tax lien, judgment lien, etc.), check the appropriate box in item 5, complete items 1-7 as applicable and attach any other items required under other law.

6. If this Financing Statement is filed as a fixture filing or if the collateral consists of timber to be cut or as-extracted collateral, complete items 1-5, check the box in item 6, and complete the required information (items 13, 14 and/or 15) on Addendum (Form UCC1Ad).

7. This item is optional. Check appropriate box in item 7 to request Search Report(s) on all or some of the Debtors named in this Financing Statement. The Report will list all Financing Statements on file against the designated Debtor on the date of the Report, including this Financing Statement. There is an additional fee for each Report. If you have checked a box in item 7, file Search Report Copy together with Filing Officer Copy (and Acknowledgment Copy). Note: Not all states do searches and not all states will honor a search request made via this form; some states require a separate request form.

8. This item is optional and is for filer's use only. For filer's convenience of reference, filer may enter in item 8 any identifying information (e.g., Secured Party's loan number, law firm file number, Debtor's name or other identification, state in which form is being filed, etc.) that filer may find useful.

Instructions for National UCC Financing Statement Addendum (Form UCC1Ad)

9. Insert name of first Debtor shown on Financing Statement to which this Addendum is related, exactly as shown in item 1 of Financing Statement.

10. Miscellaneous: Under certain circumstances, additional information not provided on Financing Statement may be required. Also, some states have non-uniform requirements. Use this space to provide such additional information or to comply with such requirements; otherwise, leave blank.

11. If this Addendum adds an additional Debtor, complete item 11 in accordance with Instruction 1 on Financing Statement. To add more than one additional Debtor, either use an additional Addendum form for each additional Debtor or replicate for each additional Debtor the formatting of Financing Statement item 1 on an 8-1/2 X 11 inch sheet (showing at the top of the sheet the name of the first Debtor shown on the Financing Statement), and in either case give complete information for each additional Debtor in accordance with Instruction 1 on Financing Statement. All additional Debtor information, especially the name, must be presented in proper format exactly identical to the format of item 1 of Financing Statement.

12. If this Addendum adds an additional Secured Party, complete item 12 in accordance with Instruction 3 on Financing Statement. In the case of a total assignment of the Secured Party's interest before the filing of this Financing Statement, if filer has given the name and address of the Total Assignee in item 3 of the Financing Statement, filer may give the Assignor S/P's name and address in item 12.

13-15. If collateral is timber to be cut or as-extracted collateral, or if this Financing Statement is filed as a fixture filing, check appropriate box in item 13; provide description of real estate in item 14; and, if Debtor is not a record owner of the described real estate, also provide, in item 15, the name and address of a record owner. Also provide collateral description in item 4 of Financing Statement. Also check box 6 on Financing Statement. Description of real estate must be sufficient under the applicable law of the jurisdiction where the real estate is located.

16. Use this space to provide continued description of collateral, if you cannot complete description in item 4 of Financing Statement.

17. If Debtor is a trust or a trustee acting with respect to property held in trust or is a decedent's estate, check the appropriate box.

18. If Debtor is a transmitting utility or if the Financing Statement relates to a Manufactured-Home Transaction or a Public-Finance Transaction as defined in the applicable Commercial Code, check the appropriate box.

GLOSSARY

abusive trust A trust designated by the IRS as suspect, intending to illegally avoid income taxes.

C corporation A regular corporation by default for income tax purposes. Pays income taxes at the corporate level, and distributions to shareholders are taxed again.

Chapter 7 bankruptcy Straight liquidation. The debtor loses most of his or her assets and debts are wiped clean.

Chapter 13 bankruptcy A wage earner's plan. Debtor repays his or her debts under a three- to five-year plan.

charging order A court order directing the manager of an LLC or the general partner of a limited partnership to assign the income of a member or partner to his or her creditor.

community property Presumption that marital property is owned by both spouses regardless of how it is titled.

contingent fee A fee arrangement by which a lawyer gets paid a portion of what he or she collects for the client.

deed in lieu of foreclosure A transfer of ownership of a property by a borrower to the lender to avoid a foreclosure.

deed of trust A security instrument under which a borrower pledges his or her property as collateral for a loan; essentially the same as a mortgage.

deficiency An amount due a lender by a borrower when a foreclosure sale yields insufficient proceeds to satisfy the mortgage debt.

discharge An order by a bankruptcy court wiping out debts.

elective share State law that allows a surviving spouse to choose whether to accept what is left to him or her under a will by the deceased or take a share (generally one-third) as prescribed by state law. Prevents a person from leaving his or her spouse little or nothing from his or her estate.

ERISA (Employee Retirement Income Security Act) ERISA-qualified pension plans are exempt from creditor attachment.

exempt property Property designated by state or federal law that cannot be taken by a creditor to satisfy a debt (a homestead, for example).

family limited partnership (FLP) A limited partnership between family members. *See* limited partnership.

foreclosure Legal process of a lender recouping the collateral for a debt.

franchise tax Annual fee charged by a state on corporations and LLCs for the privilege of doing business.

fraudulent transfer A transfer of assets intended to frustrate or defraud a creditor.

homestead exemption State law that protects one's own personal residence from creditor attachment. This exemption is generally waived as against a lender with a mortgage lien on the property.

intervivos trust A trust created during the life of the grantor (also known as a living trust).

IRA (individual retirement account) An account in which a person may deposit up to a stipulated amount each year determined by federal law and in which profits earned are not taxable. Withdrawals may be taxed, except in the case of a Roth IRA.

irrevocable trust A trust that cannot be revoked, modified, or terminated, except as provided in the trust agreement.

joint tenancy Ownership in which two or more parties hold equal and simultaneously created interests in the same property and in which title to the entire property is to remain with the survivors on the death of one of them.

land trust Revocable trust used to hold title to real estate. Also known as title-holding trust or a nominee trust.

licensee A person authorized to use the property of another under a contractual agreement.

limited liability company (LLC) A creation of state law that provides liability protection for its owners and flexible tax treatment.

limited liability partnership (LLP) A creation of state law that provides some liability protection of business owners from their partners' misconduct.

limited partnership A creation of state law that provides liability protection for limited partners (investors).

living trust A trust created during the life of the grantor (also known as an *intervivos* trust)

mortgage A security instrument under which a borrower pledges his or her property as collateral for a loan.

negligence The failure to act reasonably in light of the risk of harm.

precedent Previous court decisions on a particular topic.

promissory note A written promise to pay a debt.

S corporation A corporation electing to be treated as a pass-through entity.

security instrument A legal document that pledges property as collateral for an obligation.

statute Written law enacted by a state or federal governing body.

statute of limitations The maximum time under the law to commence a lawsuit.

strict liability Liability imposed by law without proof of fault.

tenancy by the entirety Ownership that is shared by spouses who are considered one person in law and have the rights of survivorship inherent in joint tenancy.

tenancy in common Ownership in which two or more parties share ownership of property but have no right to each other's interest on the death of another owner (tenant in common).

tortious Wrongful; pertaining to wrongdoing.

unincorporated business organization A quasicorporation formed as a trust.

VA Veterans Administration; part of the Department of Veterans Affairs.

RESOURCES

Incorporation Resource Directory

Federal Tax Forms

1-800-TAX-1040
www.irs.ustreas.gov/formspubs/index.html

State Tax Forms

http://taxes.yahoo.com/stateforms.html

Domestic Incorporation Services

www.mycorporation.com
www.incorporate.com
www.blumberg.com

Offshore Incorporation Services

Universal Corporate Services
1-800-551-9105

Corporate Seals/Kits

CorpKit Legal Supplies
1-888-888-9120
www.corpkit.com

Registered Agent Service

Blumberg/Excelsior Corporate Services
1-800-LAW-MART
www.blumberg.com
National Registered Agents, Inc.
1-877-812-6724
www.nrai.com

Important Tax and Small Business Information Web Sites

Commerce Clearing House
www.cch.com
IRS Bulletins and Tax Decisions
www.irs.ustreas.gov/businesses/index.html
Quicken Small Business
www.quicken.com/small_business
The LegalWiz
www.legalwiz.com
MSN Money Central Tax Info
http://moneycentral.msn.com/tax/home.asp

Online Corporation Departments and Secretary of State Offices

www.findlaw.com/11stategov/indexcorp.html
www.nrai.com (click on the "Research" icon)

Department of Corporations/Secretary of State Offices & Web Sites		
Alabama	Secretary of State P.O. Box 5616 Montgomery, AL 36130 334-242-5324	www.Alalinc.net/alsecst/ corporat.htm
Alaska	Division of Corps. P.O. Box 110807 Juneau, AK 99811 907-465-2521	www/state.ak.us/local/akpages/ COMMERCE/bsc/bsc.htm
Arizona	Ariz. Corp. Commission 1300 W. Washington Phoenix, AZ 85005 602-542-3135	www.cc.state.az.us
Arkansas	Secretary of State Corporation Division State Capital, Room 58 Little Rock, AR 72201 501-682-5151	www.state.ar.us/sos/index.html
California	Secretary of State Corporate Division Attn: Legal Review 1230 J Street Sacramento, CA 95814 916-657-5448	www.ss.ca.gov/
Colorado	Secretary of State Corporations Office 1560 Broadway, Suite 200 Denver, CO 80202 303-894-2251	www.state.ar.us/sos/index.html
Connecticut	Secretary of State 30 Trinity Street P.O. Box 150470 Hartford, CT 06106 203-566-4128	www.state.ct.us/sots/

Department of Corporations/Secretary of State Offices & Web Sites		
Delaware	Secretary of State, Div. of Corps. P.O. Box 898 Dover, DE 19903 302-739-3073	www.state.de.us/govern/agencies/ corp/corp.htm
Dist. of Columbia	Dept. of Consumer Affairs Sup. of Corps. 614 H Street N.W., Room 407 Washington, DC 20001 202-727-7283	www.ci.washington.dc.us/DCRA/ bracorp.htm
Florida	Secretary of State Division of Corporations P.O. Box 6327 Tallahassee, FL 32314 904-488-9000	www.dos.state.fl.us/doc
Georgia	Secretary of State 2 Martin Luther King Jr. Drive Ste. 315 – West Tower Atlanta, GA 30330 404-656-2817	www.SOS.State.Ga.US/
Hawaii	Dept. of Commerce Bus. Reg. Div. P.O. Box 40 Honolulu, HI 96810 808-586-2727	www.SOS.State.Ga.US/
Idaho	Secretary of State 700 W. Jefferson Basement West Boise, ID 83720-0080 208-334-2301	www.idsos.state.id.us/
Illinois	Secretary of State Bus. Services Dept. 328 Howlett Building Springfield, IL 62756 217-782-6961	www.Sos.state.il.us/depts.bus_serv/ bus_home.html

Department of Corporations/Secretary of State Offices & Web Sites		
Indiana	Secretary of State Room 155 State House 302 W. Washington, Room E018 Indianapolis, IN 46204 317-232-6576	
Iowa	Secretary of State Corps. Divs. Hoover Bldg. Des Moines, IA 50319 515-281-5204	www.sos.state.ia.us/
Kansas	Secretary of State Capital Building, 2nd Floor 300 S.W. 10th Street Topeka, KS 66612-1594 913-296-2236	www.state.ks.us/public/sos/
Kentucky	Office of Secretary of State P.O. Box 718 Frankfort, KY 40602 502-564-2848	www.sos.state.ky.us/
Louisiana	Secretary of State, Corp. Division P.O. Box 94125 Baton Rouge, LA 70804 504-925-4704	www.sec.state.la.us/
Maine	Secretary of State Bureau of Corps., Elections, and Commissions 101 State House Station Augusta, ME 04333 207-287-4195	www.state.me.us/sos/sos.htm
Maryland	Dept. of Assessments & Taxation 301 W. Preston Street, Rm. 809 Baltimore, MD 21201 410-767-1340	www.dat.state.md.us/charter.html

Department of Corporations/Secretary of State Offices & Web Sites		
Massachusetts	Secretary of State Corps. Division One Ashborn Place, 17th Floor Boston, MA 02108 617-727-9640	www.state.ma.us/massgov.htm

Michigan	Mich. Dept. of Commerce, Corp.
	   Securities Bureau, Corps.
	   Divisions
	P.O. Box 30054
	Lansing, MI 48909-7554
	517-334-6302
		www.sos.state.mi.us/

Minnesota	Secretary of State Division of Corps. 180 State Office Bldg. 100 Constitution Ave. St. Paul, MN 55155 612-296-2803	www.sos.state.mn.us/bus.html
Mississippi	Secretary of State Bus. Services Div. P.O. Box 136 Jackson, MS 39205 601-359-1633	www.sos.state.ms.us/
Missouri	Secretary of State, Corp. Div. P.O. Box 778 Jefferson City, MO 65102 573-751-2359	Mosl.sos.state.mo.us/bus-ser/ soscor.html
Montana	Secretary of State P.O. Box 202801 Helena, MT 59620 406-444-2034	www.mt.gov/sos/biz.htm
Nebraska	Secretary of State Suite 1301, State Capitol Lincoln, NE 68509 402-471-4079	www.nol.org/home/SOS/ services.htm

Department of Corporations/Secretary of State Offices & Web Sites		
Nevada	Secretary of State Capitol Complex Carson City, NV 89710 702-687-5203	jvm.com/sos/
New Hampshire	Secretary of State State House, Rm. 204 107 N. Main Street Concord, NH 03301 603-271-3244	
New Jersey	Secretary of State Div. of Commercial Recording Trenton, NJ 08625 609-530-6400	www.state.nj.us/state/
New Mexico	State Corp. Commission Corp. Dept. P.O. Drawer 1269 Santa Fe, NM 87504 505-827-4511	www.sos.state.nm.us/
New York	Dept. of State Div. of Corps. and State Records 162 Washington Ave. Albany, NY 12231 518-473-2494	www.dos.state.ny.us/
North Carolina	Corps. Div. Dept. of Secretary of State 300 N. Salisbury Street Raleigh, NC 27603-5909 919-733-4201	www.secstate.state.nc.us/secstate/
North Dakota	Secretary of State Capitol Building 600 E. Blvd. Ave. Bismarck, ND 58505 701-328-2900	

Department of Corporations/Secretary of State Offices & Web Sites		
Ohio	Secretary of State, Corps. Div. 30 E. Broad Street State Office Tower, 14th Fl. Columbus, OH 43266 614-466-3910	www.state.oh.us/sos/
Oklahoma	Secretary of State, Corp. Div. 101 State Capitol Building Oklahoma City, OK 73105 405-521-3911	www.occ.state.ok.us/
Oregon	Corp. Div., State of Oregon 158-12th Street N.E. Salem, OR 97310 503-986-2200	www.sos.state.or.us/
Pennsylvania	Dept. of State, Corp. Bureau P.O. Box 8722 Harrisburg, PA 17015 717-787-1057	www.state.pa.us/PA_Exec/State/
Rhode Island	Secretary of State 100 N. Main St. Providence, RI 02903 401-277-3040	www.state.ri.us/STDEPT/sdlink.htm
South Carolina	Secretary of State P.O. Box 11350 Columbia, SC 29211 803-734-2158	www.leginfo.state.sc.us/ secretary.html
South Dakota	Secretary of State, State Capitol 500 E. Capitol Pierre SD 57501 605-773-3537	www.state.sd.us/state/executive/sos/ sos.htm
Tennessee	Dept. of State Div. of Services, Suite 1800 James Polk Bldg. Nashville, TN 37243 615-741-2286	www.state.tn.us/sos/index.htm

Department of Corporations/Secretary of State Offices & Web Sites		
Texas	Secretary of State, Corp. Div. P.O. Box 13697 Austin, TX 78711 512-463-5555	www.state.tx.us/agency/307.html
Utah	Dept. of Commerce, Div. of Corps. and Commercial Code Box 45801 160 E. 300 S., 2nd Floor Salt Lake City, UT 84145 801-530-4849	www.commerce.state.ut.us/web/ commerce/corporat/corpcoc.htm
Vermont	Secretary of State 109 State Street Montpelier, VT 05609 802-828-2363	www.sec.state.vt.us/
Virginia	State Corp. Commission Jefferson Building P.O. Box 1197 Richmond, VA 23219 804-371-9733	www.state.va.us/scc/index.html
Washington	Secretary of State, Corp. Div. P.O. Box 40234 Olympia, WA 98504 360-753-7115	www.wa.gov/sec/
West Virginia	Secretary of State, State Capitol Charleston, WV 25305 304-558-8000	
Wisconsin	Sec. of State, Corp. Div. P.O. Box 7846 Madison, WI 53707 608-266-3590	
Wyoming	Secretary of State State Capitol Building Cheyenne, WY 82002 307-777-7311	Soswy.state.wy.us/

Suggested Reading

Asset Protection for Physicians and High-Risk Business Owners by Robert J. Mintz (Francis O'Brien and Sons, 1999)

Asset Protection Secrets by Arnold S. Goldstein (Commonwealth Publications, 1997)

How to Create a Bulletproof Corporation by William Bronchick (LegalWiz Publications, <www.legalwiz.com>)

Settle Your Tax Debt: How to Save Thousands Using the IRS Offer-in-Compromise Program by Sean P. Melvin (Dearborn Trade, 1998)

Tax Savvy for Small Business by Frederick W. Daily (Nolo Press, 2002)

The Business Turnaround and Bankruptcy Kit by John Ventura (Dearborn Trade, 2003)

The Complete Book of Trusts by Martin M. Shenkman (Wiley, 1997)

The Limited Liability Company Reporter by Phil Whynot (James Publishing)

The Riser Report (free bimonthly newsletter), <http://www.riserreport .com/>

Using Land Trusts for Privacy & Protection by William Bronchick (LegalWiz Publications, <www.legalwiz.com>)

<www.legalwiz.com>

The #1 Legal and Financial Internet Resource for Small Business and Real Estate Entrepreneurs

- **Audio and Video Downloads**
- **Dozens of New Articles Each Month**
- **FREE Legal Forms**
- **FREE Newsletter**
- **Legal and Real Estate Dictionary**
- **"Ask the LegalWiz" Interactive Message Board**
- **Links to Hundreds of Legal and Real Estate Sites**
- **New Product Information and Updates**
- **Sample Asset Protection Plans**
- **Seminar Information and Registration**
- **Online Product Ordering**

<www.legalwiz.com>

Hosted by Attorney William Bronchick

INDEX

Share the message!

Bulk discounts
Discounts start at only 10 copies. Save up to 55% off retail price.

Custom publishing
Private label a cover with your organization's name and logo.
Or, tailor information to your needs with a custom pamphlet
that highlights specific chapters.

Ancillaries
Workshop outlines, videos, and other products are available on
select titles.

Dynamic speakers
Engaging authors are available to share their expertise and insight
at your event.

Call Dearborn Trade Special Sales at
1-800-245-BOOK (2665)
or e-mail trade@dearborn.com

Dearborn™
Trade Publishing
A **Kaplan Professional** Company